PENGUIN

# RANDY BACHMAN'S VINYL TAP STORIES

RANDY BACHMAN has become a legendary figure in the rock 'n' roll world through his talent as a guitarist, songwriter, performer, and producer. Best known for his work in the Guess Who and Bachman-Turner Overdrive, he has earned more than 120 gold and platinum album/singles awards around the world for performing and producing.

# RANDY BACHMAN'S
## Vinyl Tap Stories

Randy Bachman

PENGUIN
an imprint of Penguin Canada

Published by the Penguin Group
Penguin Group (Canada), 90 Eglinton Avenue East, Suite 700,
Toronto, Ontario, Canada M4P 2Y3 (a division of Pearson Canada Inc.)

Penguin Group (USA) Inc., 375 Hudson Street, New York, New York 10014, U.S.A.
Penguin Books Ltd, 80 Strand, London WC2R 0RL, England
Penguin Ireland, 25 St Stephen's Green, Dublin 2, Ireland
(a division of Penguin Books Ltd)
Penguin Group (Australia), 250 Camberwell Road, Camberwell, Victoria 3124, Australia
(a division of Pearson Australia Group Pty Ltd)
Penguin Books India Pvt Ltd, 11 Community Centre, Panchsheel Park,
New Delhi – 110 017, India
Penguin Group (NZ), 67 Apollo Drive, Rosedale, Auckland 0632, New Zealand
(a division of Pearson New Zealand Ltd)
Penguin Books (South Africa) (Pty) Ltd, 24 Sturdee Avenue, Rosebank,
Johannesburg 2196, South Africa

Penguin Books Ltd, Registered Offices: 80 Strand, London WC2R 0RL, England

First published in Viking hardcover by Penguin Canada,
a division of Pearson Canada Inc., 2011
Published in this edition, 2012

1 2 3 4 5 6 7 8 9 10 (WEB)

Copyright © Randy Bachman, 2011

Manufactured in Canada.

LIBRARY AND ARCHIVES CANADA CATALOGUING IN PUBLICATION

Bachman, Randy, 1943–
Randy Bachman's Vinyl tap stories / Randy Bachman.

Includes discographies and index.
ISBN 978-0-14-318040-1

1. Bachman, Randy, 1943– —Anecdotes. 2. Rock
music—Anecdotes. I. Title. II. Title: Vinyl tap stories.

ML420.B113A3 2012       782.42166092       C2012-903806-7

Visit the Penguin Canada website at **www.penguin.ca**

Special and corporate bulk purchase rates available; please see
**www.penguin.ca/corporatesales** or call 1-800-810-3104, ext. 2477.

ALWAYS LEARNING                                                    PEARSON

# Contents

# Introduction

*Born and raised in a prairie town*
*Just a kid full of dreams*
*We didn't have much but an old radio*
*Music came from places we'd never been*
*Growing up in a prairie town*
*Learning to drive in the snow*
*Not much to do so you start a band*
*And soon you've gone as far as you can go*
*Winter nights are long, summer days are gone*
*Portage & Main fifty below*
*Springtime melts the snow, rivers overflow*
*Portage & Main fifty below*
—"PRAIRIE TOWN" BY RANDY BACHMAN

Radio was my lifeline as a kid growing up in Winnipeg in the 1950s. It connected me with the wider world outside our little prairie city and offered me my first introduction to rock 'n' roll and the guitar sounds and styles I wanted to play. Radio gave me my life's direction. It's been a constant for me no matter where I've lived.

Long before MTV, MuchMusic, the internet, or iTunes, teenagers tuned in to their radios to hear the message of rock 'n' roll. And I was one of them. Whether you grew up in a big city like Toronto or Vancouver or a little town in Saskatchewan or Nova Scotia, I'm sure you can all remember the first time you heard rock 'n' roll on the radio. Growing up in Winnipeg, the first time I heard it was on the two local radio stations, CKY and CKRC. And because Winnipeg is located at the top of the Great Plains, I would go to bed at night with my little rocket radio and tune in to WLS in Chicago, WNOE in New Orleans, or places far away like Shreveport, Memphis, or Wichita that sounded exotic to a prairie boy. These stations played rock 'n' roll. The next day at school, the topic of conversation among my friends was along the lines of "I picked up Des Moines, Iowa, on the radio last night and they played 'Rock Around the Clock'!" My parents would yell at me to turn my radio off and go to bed, so I'd take it under the covers and carry on with my nightly ritual. Just like kids nowadays surfing the internet, in the 50s I surfed the radio dial. I remember hearing Chuck Berry's "School Days" for the first time and being completely blown away. I'd never heard guitar like that.

But unlike most teenagers, I went from listening to the radio to being heard on radio, making records that would actually get played by a deejay. You can't imagine the thrill of hearing yourself on the radio for the first time.

Playing in a band in Winnipeg, I got to know many of the local radio deejays at CKY and CKRC, guys not much older than me like Doc Steen, Boyd Kozak, Dino Corrie, Daryl B., Jim Christie, PJ the DJ. They were cool because they got to talk on the radio and play records, the records I loved to hear. So even though I was playing in a popular band, making records, and becoming well known, I still envied them and their gig. (Who knows, they probably envied me for being in a band.) They got to spin the discs and do all the "platter chatter." But I never dreamed that one day I'd be on the radio spinning those discs and sharing my stories.

In more recent years, I used to listen to *Finkleman's 45s* on CBC Radio when I was home on a Saturday night. Danny Finkleman was a fellow Winnipegger and often told stories about growing up in the North End of the city, the area I came from. I'd met him once or twice at the CBC in Winnipeg when the Guess Who was the house band on CBC-TV's *Let's Go* back in 1967–68. But when I heard he was retiring, I thought to myself, "Why would anyone want to quit playing records and talking once a week for a couple of hours? Who wouldn't kill to have that gig?" So I told my wife, Denise, "What's so hard about doing what he's doing? I could do that. And I love to share my stories and experiences."

Like a lot of events in my life, things just happen. No master plan or calculation; they just happen. I owe as much to serendipity as I do to premeditation in my career. Three of the biggest hits I've been associated with—"American Woman," "Takin' Care of Business," and "You Ain't Seen Nothing Yet"—all sprang from happenstance, a moment in time. I've learned to accept that when opportunities present themselves, you have to grab them because they don't come around again. So I decided to take a shot at being a radio deejay on CBC. Trouble is, I had no idea how to go about letting the powers that be know that.

I wrote a letter to the CBC—no one specific, just the CBC—explaining my concept, and I gave it to one of the technicians when I was a guest on Stuart McLean's *Vinyl Cafe* radio show. He later passed it along to Jennifer McGuire, at the time the head of CBC's English-language radio programming. Here's what I wrote in the letter:

Dear CBC Radio,

   I'm a big fan of CBC Radio. This past Saturday's show of *Finkleman's 45s* I noticed that Danny said he was retiring. I would love his time slot, and my proposal is that I play music from my own record collection and tell personal stories about the artist, song, etc. Instead of *Finkleman's 45s* you could call the show *Randy's Rockin' Records* or *Randy Bachman's Vinyl Tap*, like *Spinal Tap*.

                                        *from Randy Bachman*

Jennifer contacted me and thought the idea was terrific. So we arranged a demo of the show just to see how I would come across on the radio. At the first session I was all over the place, yelling "Whoa! Yeah, baby! Let's rock!" like Wolfman Jack, and speed-jiving like crazy. It was way over the top, and CBC producer Chris Boyce suggested I simmer down a bit. After all, it's an early evening show. When I was a kid in Winnipeg, CKY had a smooth-talking deejay named Richard Scott who spoke in this low, sexy, resonating tone to all the housewives every afternoon, cooing, "Hello, kitten. Relax. Light up a cigarette. It's just you and me." So I tried that approach, but they thought it was too mellow. We did several more attempts at finding the right "voice," pacing, and style for the show until we finally hit on the right formula. The trick was to tape the shows after dinner when I was a bit mellower and laid-back. No shrieking or hushed whispers.

*Randy Bachman's Vinyl Tap* debuted as a summer replacement show in 2005, and it was such a hit that the CBC ran it again in reruns over the fall and signed me to a contract to do the series beginning in 2006. After doing the show alone, I realized I needed some help. Denise came on board, answering all the emails and real mail we started getting, which makes the listeners and people who write in all feel like part of the *Vinyl Tap* family. Her mailbag segment has tons of fans. When we poll the audience about something like the first records they ever bought, Denise sorts out all the responses and then reads each person's little story. I then add facts about the music or performer. Denise also does the research, so that when I tell a personal story that relates to the music, she has already provided me with correct dates, names, places, etc. to put my stories into proper context. It all works organically and synergistically. Since the beginning, the format has evolved only slightly because it works as it is. Denise loves music and has her own eclectic musical tastes, which balance out mine. We complement each other very well, and it keeps the show moving at a good pace.

Putting together a show takes us many hours of listening to music, getting the original or best performance of the song, and finding ones for which I know something about the artist, writer, producer, or musicians so that I can tell an original story. We then sequence the songs in a strategic order (like a stage show) and I burn a CD for Tod Elvidge, our producer. Denise prints out the info, I get a guitar, and we usually record three shows at a sitting.

Denise is the only other voice on *Vinyl Tap*. CBC didn't want it to be a show that featured guests. They wanted it to be all me, my song choices and stories. CBC and I agree that it's really about my storytelling. The music is secondary to that. It's my ability to give an insider perspective and personal insight, experience, and knowledge about the music that is the strength of *Vinyl Tap*. I have so many ideas for concepts and so many stories to share with listeners. I love doing the show and hope to continue the fun and the run for many years.

One of the great features of *Vinyl Tap* has been the feedback we receive from our listeners. We get emails and letters from around the world. Sometimes some of the fact junkies take me to task about a date or fact I got wrong, and that's cool. I'm not perfect. For me, it's the story that matters, not the exact date. Often we get suggestions for themes for future shows, many of which we've followed up on.

Some of my favourite themes have been "Mondegreens" (Denise's idea), "From Demos to Hits," "The Cowbell Show," and "Guitarology 101."

I never realized the amount of work involved in preparing a radio show. In my naïveté I just thought I would show up with an armful of vinyl, 45s and albums, play them and talk in between. Not so. But once I got into the rhythm of doing the shows, it was great fun. Initially I taped the shows at my home recording studio in the Gulf Islands, but now we do it at CBC's studio in Victoria. For thousands of Canadians and millions of listeners on Sirius

Satellite Radio, their Saturday night routine involves tuning in to *Vinyl Tap*. I'm very proud of that and I don't take the responsibility lightly.

What started as a summer replacement series has turned into a wonderful thing for me. It's a dream come true. After more than forty years in rock 'n' roll, I've finally got a real job.

Over the years many people have asked me when I was going to collect many of the stories I've shared on the show in a book. Well, for all those who asked and for all the other *Randy Bachman's Vinyl Tap* listeners, here it is. Enjoy!

*Randy Bachman's Vinyl Tap Stories*

# Portage and Main

Winnipeg is a working-class city that breeds a toughness and durability in its inhabitants. It's a city of extremes. The winters are brutally cold and long while the summers tend to be hot, humid, and mosquito infested. In between is the occasional flood. But for those born and raised in Winnipeg, the city never leaves you, no matter where you go. Although I haven't lived in Winnipeg since 1972, it is and always will be my home and hometown. The thing about Winnipeg is that it's built on two rivers, the Red and Assiniboine, and the two big important streets follow those rivers: Main Street follows the Red River and Portage Avenue follows the Assiniboine. Where they meet is just behind Portage and Main, the centre of Winnipeg. That was the most famous intersection in the city because not only did it follow the meeting of the rivers but you would also change buses there going from one end of the city to the other. And that was also where all the radio stations were and all the big buildings downtown began. So Portage and Main meant a lot of things to me growing up. I remember that when the Winnipeg Jets hockey team signed "The Golden Jet" Bobby Hull, they did it at Portage and Main, and thousands of Winnipeggers blocked the intersection to witness the event.

In 1993 I wrote a song about growing up in Winnipeg entitled "Prairie Town," and in the chorus I sang, "Portage and Main, fifty below." As a kid in Winnipeg I would pass by Portage and Main, and right at the intersection there was a great big Coca-Cola sign that flashed the time and the temperature all day long, back and forth. So you'd pass by on the bus or in your car and see "8:25 a.m." and then "45 below 0." And the radio stations there would simply say, "The time is …" and look out the window at the Coca-Cola sign. Then they'd say, "And the temperature at Portage and Main is …" So when I wrote "Prairie Town" I remembered that sign and put in the line "Portage and Main, fifty below."

Music was always such a big part of my life growing up in Winnipeg. My parents wanted their children to play a musical instrument. We couldn't afford a piano, so my older brother Gary was given an accordion and I received a little half-size violin. I wasn't even school age yet, but I started taking violin lessons. I remember my first day of school and the teacher asking everyone what they wanted to be when they grew up. Of course you had the typical responses like bus driver, nurse, and fireman. When it came to my turn, I said "musician" because I'd already been playing violin. As far as I was concerned that was who I was and wanted to be.

After about a year of lessons in the neighbourhood, I got a different teacher and was required to ride the bus to his house. Alone. I was six or seven years old and I couldn't even read the street signs. So I'd look for the toy soldiers outside Toyland at Eaton's Portage Avenue department store, get off the bus with my green transfer in my hand, and wait there right downtown all alone for a bus that had "Cor" on it. I could read that much. That was the Corydon bus, and I would take it all the way to the south of Winnipeg until I saw a big school and playground. I would get off the bus and walk two blocks to Mr. Rutherford's house for a one-hour lesson. Then I retraced my steps, transferring at Eaton's to my bus, which took me near my home in West Kildonan in the

North End. I'd walk the rest of the way home. I did this every Saturday. I didn't even know where I was going, but I remember my parents telling me not to daydream on the bus because I might miss my stop: "Pay attention!" Every Saturday I was terrified I might miss my stop, and then what would I do?

One Saturday that happened. I wasn't paying attention and I missed getting off at the toy soldiers. Crying, I ran to the driver. "Stop! Take me back to the soldiers! I have to get off at the soldiers!"

"I can't," he told me. "It's a trolley bus. It doesn't back up."

I thought I was lost forever and would never see my parents and my house again. The driver managed to stop the bus in the middle of the street and let me off. Here I was, this hysterical little kid with a violin case, walking back to the toy soldiers. As I'm walking I look up and see the Corydon bus pass me by. I was panicking because in my mind I thought that was the only "Cor" bus and I'd missed it. Nowadays even little kids have cell phones. I had nothing. I didn't know where I was going or even how to get home. So I started running after the bus. The driver saw me and stopped to let me on. He recognized me, the little kid with the violin from every Saturday morning. The sheer terror of that moment has never left me. It astounds me to this day that a six-year-old kid rode the bus in a big city like Winnipeg all alone. I would never let my kids or grandkids do that today.

But of course, I wasn't going to be playing the violin forever. Music was changing. There was a television commercial a few years ago that I used to get a kick out of watching. It was of a young boy, supposedly Jimi Hendrix, looking in the window of an accordion store, and across the street is a guitar store. He's trying to decide which one to go with: accordion or guitar. I think the commercial was for a soft drink, but it was one of those ads that are more than the product. In the background someone is playing Hendrix's "Purple Haze" on an accordion. I can relate to that scene. Can you imagine hearing "Takin' Care of Business" on a violin?

My mother always had the radio on around the house. I grew up with the radio. We didn't even have a television for several years. My brothers and I would come home at lunch and tune into CKY or CKRC for a whole hour listening to rock 'n' roll. Country music was still big in Winnipeg and the Prairies, but they were starting to play rock 'n' roll.

I used to go to all the country-and-western package shows at the Winnipeg Auditorium to see the fiddle players. Ray Price, Patsy Cline—they all had great fiddle players. On one occasion they introduced this fellow with neat curly blond hair who sat down at the piano and played "You Win Again" and a Johnny Cash song. Then he jumped up, kicked the piano stool aside, and started pounding "Whole Lotta Shakin' Goin' On" with his hair falling over his face. It was Jerry Lee Lewis. I'd never seen anything like him. It was a country show where people sat there and politely applauded Kitty Wells or Patsy Cline. The next day on CKRC, Doug Burrows played "Whole Lotta Shakin' Goin' On." Rock 'n' roll was just catching fire in Winnipeg, and the phones lit up. So he played it again back to back. I was mesmerized.

I had a friend, Shelly Ostrove, whose dad was an electrician, and they had the first television set on the block; it was black-and-white TV only back then. Needless to say Shelly's place was *the* place to go after school for all us kids to watch *Range Rider* and *Howdy Doody*. One Sunday night I got invited to his house to watch *The Ed Sullivan Show* and saw Elvis Presley for the first time. That moment inspired me. It was the first time I heard "Tutti Frutti." Forget the violin, I wanted to play this!

My brother Gary had some friends who went to the ProTeen club, a teen dance hall on Pritchard Avenue off Arlington Street in the North End, a really hip spot for dancers. His friends had dropped out of school and were working so that they could afford the coolest clothes. They were way hipper than I was. Gary brought them over one day and they said to me, "You like Elvis's 'Tutti Frutti'?"

"Yeah!" I told them.

"Have you heard Little Richard?"

"No. Who's that?"

"He's the guy that wrote 'Tutti Frutti.'"

So the next weekend they brought over a Little Richard album, and man, if I thought Elvis was wild, this was out of this world. Ten times wilder, screaming and shrieking. I'd never heard anything like it, the ferocity of that sound. When I played classical violin, it was all very structured and formal, playing the notes on the page written hundreds of years before. Now to hear rock 'n' roll and hear the freedom in the notes and playing was liberating to me.

Once I started playing guitar, I would sit by the radio with my Silvertone guitar and try to play these incredible songs. At night I'd be playing guitar in the bedroom that I shared with Gary, and when my parents would tell me to turn the lights out and go to bed, I'd turn off the lights but continue playing. That's why I got so good at not having to look at my fretboard when I played, because I learned to play in the dark. I remember Gary telling me that one evening he went out with his friends—I guess it was a weekend—and left me playing guitar on my bed. When he came home after midnight, I was still in the same spot and the same position playing my guitar.

My cousins, the Dupas brothers, lived out in the town of La Broquerie near Woodridge, southeast of Winnipeg. They had a blond, jumbo-sized Gibson hollow-body electric guitar, the kind Scotty Moore and Chuck Berry played. It was the coolest instrument I'd ever seen. While the grown-ups would be visiting, these guys would let me play their guitar and show me things. They would teach me Johnny Cash songs because they were into country music. Years later I bought that guitar from them.

I've played thousands of gigs in my career, but never one as memorable as my public debut where I was upstaged by a Christmas tree.

Garry Peterson and I went to Edmund Partridge Junior High on Main Street in West Kildonan. For the Christmas show, we put a band together called the Embers with another schoolmate of mine named Perry Waksvik. We were going to play Buddy Knox's "Rockabilly Walk." The curtain opens and Garry starts to play the drums. He's set up in front of this giant decorated Christmas tree. I emerge from behind the curtain playing my guitar, and the crowd gasps. I thought to myself, "Wow, am I cool with my Elvis wave in my hair and my cool guitar!" I thought they were gasping for me. Instead they were gasping because the cord for my guitar was tangled in the giant Christmas tree and I was pulling it over, about to topple it on Garry and his drums. Thank god someone grabbed the tree and unplugged it in time before it crashed down on Garry. Needless to say I didn't get to play my big song at the Christmas show. The teachers stopped it and sent us off the stage. All my buddies applauded and yelled out, "Yay for Bachman!"

In the 1960s, Winnipeg was the rock 'n' roll capital of Canada. It was like a mini Liverpool. We didn't know it at the time, but in hindsight you realize that Winnipeg was the hotbed of Canadian rock. It must have been something in the water, or in the cold. We grew up with different ethnic communities throughout the city, and in every neighbourhood there was a community club. As a kid you played sports at your community club, whether hockey or baseball. And when rock 'n' roll came along, if you had a band and could play a few songs, you could get a gig playing your own community club. All your friends from school would come out and dance to the music you were making. I started out playing records at my community club before graduating to playing there in bands.

Community clubs were a big deal for us, and so was radio. I was fortunate early on in my career to meet Lenny Breau, who was working with his parents, Hal Lone Pine and Betty Cody. They had a rockabilly kind of country show and wore all those Roy Rogers and Dale Evans fringed cowboy shirts with cactuses on them. They were called the CKY Caravan and worked out of CKY radio. They even had their own Elvis Presley. He was Ray St. Germain and he was fantastic, with the Elvis pompadour and the big sideburns. I loved this guy. He recorded his first single at CKY radio in 1958, an Elvis-style rockabilly number called "She's a Square" that featured Lenny Breau on guitar. That was the first real rock 'n' roll record cut in Winnipeg. In fact, radio stations were the first places to record rock 'n' roll. There were no professional studios at the time.

My first recording experience was backing a shoe salesman from Portage la Prairie named Gary Cooper. He was a lot like Ray St. Germain and drove a big white 1959 Ford Galaxie. He rented CKY's studio, hired me to play lead guitar, and brought in the Triads to do the doo-wop backing vocals. Garry Peterson played the drums. Garry and I were in the Velvetones at the time with Mickey Brown. Gary Cooper had to change his name because of the actor of that name, so he became Gary Andrews for his recordings. We recorded "Come On Pretty Baby" with me on guitar. That was in 1961. I was eighteen.

Every city has its hip spot where teenagers congregate, and back in the 60s, Winnipeg was no exception. When I started playing in bands, the Paddlewheel restaurant on the sixth floor of the downtown Hudson's Bay department store on Portage Avenue was the coolest place to hang out and be seen.

Every Saturday my friends and I used to do the walk between Eaton's and the Bay downtown on Portage Avenue. I think everybody did, no matter what part of the city you came from. Within that five-block strip were all the hippest clothing stores and coolest restaurants, along with record shops, movie theatres, and musical instrument dealers. We would spend Saturday afternoons on that strip checking out the guitars and amps at Winnipeg Piano, buying records at the Record Room or Lillian Lewis Records, and trying on Mod clothes at the Stag Shop beside the Rialto

Theatre. The Guess Who bought all their stage clothes from Bob McGregor at the Stag Shop along the Portage strip.

But we'd always end up at the Paddlewheel. All the bands would be there on a Saturday afternoon, and our fans would be fawning over us. The radio stations sometimes did live broadcasts from the Wheel. The decor hadn't changed in decades (in fact, it's still the same!) and the food wasn't exactly haute cuisine, but for some reason teens congregated there and made it hip. I can remember saying to kids at a Friday night community club dance, "See you at the Paddlewheel tomorrow." Besides meeting your fans, that's where all the bands would catch up with each other and find out what we were all doing, where the good and bad gigs were, what new songs were being played, or who was in or out of a lineup. Because you were gigging all the time, you rarely got the chance to hang out together and compare notes.

CKY and CKRC were great stations, and really supported the local music scene. The deejays at these stations—PJ the DJ, Doc Steen, Boyd Kozak, Dino Corrie, Daryl B., Harry Taylor—were the Wolfman Jacks or Dick Clarks of the local scene. They'd go to the sock hops and emcee them, playing records and giving away 45s. These guys would promote dances on the radio all week long and work with the bands at the dances. You were really, really lucky if you had a deejay working with your band.

It was like one big family in the Winnipeg music scene. We shared amplifiers and instruments, went to each other's gigs, and hung out together. Neil Young used to borrow Jim Kale's Fender Concert amp from us whenever we weren't playing. I made friends with CKRC's Doc Steen. I'd pop in every week and Doc would give me a box of 45s that they weren't playing anymore or that didn't fit in with their format. I got some great records that way. I remember a Nina Simone 45 that was very cool called "I Loves You, Porgy," but I loved the flip side, "Love Me or Leave Me." I always thought Nina Simone was some cool

French chick, but she was a black classically trained pianist and singer from North Carolina.

By the early 60s the music scene really changed, from rockabilly, doo-wop, and Elvis to rock groups—and the best of them seemed to come from Great Britain. Beatlemania hit Winnipeg hard. All of a sudden everything was Beatles and the British Invasion.

I loved the Beatles. So when the first Beatles movie, *A Hard Day's Night,* opened in Winnipeg at the Garrick Theatre in the summer of 1964, I was right there on opening day. I went with a few friends for the matinee, and in those days you didn't have to leave the theatre between shows. My friends went home but I stayed, mesmerized, memorizing everything. I completely lost track of time. It was like a how-to video for me: how to be a rock 'n' roll star. How to run from crowds of screaming girls, how to write songs in a boxcar, how to be cheeky to a reporter. Sitting in that darkened theatre, I decided that this was what I wanted to do for the rest of my life. I must have seen the movie five or six times when I felt a tap on my shoulder. It was Phil Brown, the chief of police in West Kildonan, and my dad, who was an alderman in West Kildonan. They'd been out looking for me after the other boys had returned home and I hadn't. My dad had phoned the hospitals and the police were looking for me. They decided to go check the theatre, and there I was, immersed in Beatlemania.

When the Beatles first appeared on the scene, John Lennon played harmonica on several of their early recordings, including "Love Me Do" and "There's a Place." So I decided I would learn to play the harmonica, and began listening to and watching other guys. I ended up playing harmonica on some of the early Guess Who records, like "I Should Have Realized" and "Use Your Imagination."

One thing about the harmonica is that you have to keep it wet or the reeds dry up and you can't get any sound from them. You can blow your guts out, but all you get is tweets or nothing at all. If you've ever seen Neil Young when he's doing a solo acoustic show, he keeps his harmonicas in glasses of water on stage with him. That keeps them lubricated and easier to slide around on your lips, because of course they're made of metal and wood. When Neil needs one, he just pulls it out of the glass, shakes off the excess water, and puts it in his harmonica holder.

So there I was, the lead guitarist and harmonica player in the Guess Who. It was winter in Winnipeg, thirty below zero, and I was going off to band practice one morning. When it's that cold you have to let your car warm up awhile before you put it in gear and drive. The engine and the oil in it have to warm up. So while I'm waiting, I decide I'll use the time to practise. I pick up one of my harmonicas that's been sitting in a freezing car all night, and guess what happens? I put it to my lips and it sticks to my tongue because it's frozen metal and my mouth is wet and warm. It's like when you were a kid and your parents told you not to put your tongue on a light standard or a metal fence. So I had to go in the house with this harmonica stuck in my mouth and run hot water over it until it dislodged from my tongue. When it did so, it ripped the skin off the front top of my tongue. I couldn't play harmonica again for several months.

So remember: If you play harmonica, don't store it in the fridge or freezer or a car in winter.

At the same time as the Beatles' *A Hard Day's Night* was playing at the Garrick Theatre, the Beatles themselves paid the city a surprise visit. Their airplane landed in Winnipeg on its way to San Francisco, where the group was set to start its first full North American tour. It was a routine stop to refuel in those days because those planes couldn't make it from the U.K. to California without refuelling. It was supposed to be no big deal, but the rock 'n' roll radio stations in the city, CKY and CKRC, got wind that the Beatles would be here in Winnipeg and announced it on air. Within half an hour there were what seemed like a thousand screaming kids at the airport. In those days you could stand outside on the roof of the airport building to watch planes take off or land, so there were all these kids up there and on the ground beside the tarmac. The Beatles weren't supposed to get off the plane, but when they saw the screaming, waving mob, Brian Epstein, their manager, convinced them to come to the door and maybe come down the portable stairs that were quickly wheeled up to the plane.

Bob Burns, the host of *Teen Dance Party* on CJAY TV and our manager at the time, became the first Canadian media person to interview the Beatles in Canada. He rushed up to John Lennon and said, "Bob Burns from CJAY TV," and John replied, "That's not my problem."

The plane stayed about twenty minutes, but before it left, Bruce Decker, who was a guitar player in the Deverons with Burton Cummings, broke away from the crowd on the ground and ran toward the steps to the plane. As the crowd cheered him on, the RCMP chased him. He managed to get a few steps up the stairs before he was tackled by a Mountie and taken away. The event made the front page of the papers and even the television news the next day and was called Decker's Dash. Bruce Decker later joined the Guess Who on rhythm guitar for a few months in the summer of 1966.

The Beatles were big in Winnipeg, but so was another band, only they were from California, not Liverpool. I remember hearing the Beach Boys singing about something called surfing. I had no idea what it was; it wasn't something we did at Winnipeg Beach or Grand Beach. You'd see their albums with these boards strapped to the top of these hot rod cars and think, "What's that all about? Do people stand on these boards in the water?" I didn't have a clue.

We were all freezing in a typical Winnipeg winter. One day I'm listening to CKRC radio and Doc Steen starts describing this new craze in California called surfing. You get a board, float out onto the ocean, wait for a wave, and then you stand on the board and float as the wave carries you to shore. He said that everyone is going to California to do this and that a bunch of brothers named Wilson have gotten together and written songs about it. So I'm listening to this and imagining a board from a fence or a plank. Is it like skiing or riding a toboggan rolling downhill? It was hard to imagine guys floating on a piece of wood and standing up on a wave. I finally found out what surfing was all about, although I never tried it. But the Beach Boys started the surfing music trend.

The surfers pictured on the albums would have an old Ford station wagon with the wood panelling on the sides, and that became known as a Woody. Then they started singing about cars and a little Deuce Coupe. That's a 1932 two-door, cut down and built into a hot rod with a big chrome engine. I remember seeing Yardbirds guitarist Jeff Beck with one in a photograph. He was into these American hot rods.

The Beach Boys became the embodiment of California, with songs about surfing, girls, and cars. They were the ultimate American band. They had that barbershop-quartet kind of singing, but with a lot of cool things going on, like playing jazz notes and singing jazz bass lines. That was all Brian Wilson. He put the *Little Deuce Coupe* album together because he wanted all his car songs on one album. But that surfing thing, what did we know about that in the Prairies?

With all this music going on in my life, it's no wonder I was failing at school. Not long ago we received a letter at *Vinyl Tap* from Alex Whibley in Australia. He was in my grade 10 class at West Kildonan Collegiate in Winnipeg. He asked if I remembered him, and I do. I also remember that I got thrown out of West Kildonan Collegiate for playing hangman with my friend Dennis Tkatch, that little game where you guess the letters in the alphabet. I was called into the principal's office, and O.V. Jewitt expelled me and Dennis. Mind you, I was failing because I didn't attend very regularly; I was too busy playing guitar. I ended up going to a new school, Garden City Collegiate. That was the only school that would take me.

Fast-forward to 2006 and I get a call to come back to West Kildonan Collegiate, the new West Kildonan Collegiate. They're naming the new performing arts centre after me. So there you go. The principal who threw me out, O.V. Jewitt, is long dead now, but I know he's up there listening. So for you, Mr. Jewitt: "I made it!"

## *My Picks*

"CAN'T BUY ME LOVE" by the Beatles

"GOOD ROCKIN' TONIGHT" by Elvis Presley

"I SHOULD HAVE REALIZED" by the Guess Who

"LOVE ME DO" by the Beatles

"PLEASE PLEASE ME" by the Beatles

"PRAIRIE TOWN" by Randy Bachman with Neil Young

"TUTTI FRUTTI" by Little Richard

"WHEN I GROW UP TO BE A MAN" by the Beach Boys

"WHEN I WAS JUST A KID" by Randy Bachman
from the album *Survivor*

# What's in a Name?

I've been fortunate to be associated with two of Canada's greatest rock bands. In the mid 60s, the Guess Who put Winnipeg on the national music map with "Shakin' All Over" and helped create a national music scene. By the end of the decade we'd become international stars, scoring gold records in the U.S., including a coveted #1 single with "American Woman." Bachman-Turner Overdrive's brand of hard-driving rock would earn us gold and platinum records around the world. The Guess Who and BTO earned their acclaim; no one handed it to us on a silver platter. I'm proud of the achievements of both those bands.

Back in 1962 in Winnipeg, I was asked to join a group called Allan and the Silvertones, led by Allan Kowbel. The name was later changed to Chad Allan and the Reflections. We copied hit parade music and played dances all over Winnipeg. We tried writing our own music, and believe me, it's like anybody trying to write their first song. It was pretty bad. So we had to copy American music, and if we wanted to record an old American R&B song, someone else always seemed to beat us to it.

Back in the early 60s, once your band played your neighbourhood community club, high school, and maybe nearby community clubs in your part of the city, then you would venture further afield and play in other neighbourhoods. Neil Young and the Squires started out in Crescentwood/River Heights in south Winnipeg but began to branch out, playing in St. Vital and in the North End. The Reflections played at Crescentwood Community Club and River Heights Community Club, Neil's stomping grounds. The scene became Winnipeg-wide. It wasn't long before we were the top band in the city.

Chad Allan (Allan Kowbel) had a friend whose cousin in England would every so often mail him tapes of songs from the U.K. hit parade, and he'd bring them over to listen to. To us, the songs sounded so exotic and different from the American music we heard on the radio. On one particular tape we heard this song called "Shakin' All Over," and we decided to record it. Later, one night in December 1964, we pulled up with all our gear in our station wagon to CJAY TV Channel 7 studios beside the Polo Park shopping mall. This wasn't a recording studio; it was a TV station with one microphone in the middle of the room. We set up our amplifiers and drums around this one microphone and recorded "Shakin' All Over."

We sent the tape to the label we were signed to, Quality Records in Toronto. The head of A&R (artist and repertoire) for the label, George Struth, phoned us up and told us that he loved the record and thought it was a hit, but that he didn't want to put our name on it. By then we were known as Chad Allan and the Expressions; we'd had to change our name after an American group named the Reflections scored a hit with "Just Like Romeo and Juliet." But we weren't sure if we'd keep the Expressions name, and we hadn't yet cleared it legally. So George decided instead just to put a white label on the 45 with the words "Guess Who?" on it and send it out to radio stations. He told us that our recording had a very British sound to it and that he wanted to release it right away. "We'll let people guess who you are. That way they'll think you're a mystery British group. We'll start this rumour that this is a recording by some guys from various British bands, like one Rolling Stone, two Beatles, one Shadow. They couldn't put their names on it for contractual reasons so they simply labelled it 'Guess Who?'" It really did sound like a British record. The trick worked, and the record went to #1 across Canada.

That's how we got our name the Guess Who, even though we didn't want it. George Struth phoned us and said, "We've got your new name. It's Guess Who!" We told him we hated it! Chad was particularly disappointed that his name was now omitted.

### SCEPTER RECORDS IN NEW YORK

In the spring of 1965, after "Shakin' All Over" had been a hit across Canada, George Struth licensed the record to an American label, Scepter Records, based in New York. Scepter was primarily a black music label with artists like the Crystals, Dionne Warwick, and the Shirelles, but they also had the Kingsmen. The Kingsmen's "Louie Louie" had been a million-selling single in 1963. Scepter Records released our version of "Shakin' All Over" in the U.S. and it began climbing the Billboard singles charts in June, rising to #22. The Guess Who became the first Winnipeg group to chart internationally.

I remember I used to go down to Kresge's, a five-and-dime store next to the Eaton's store downtown, every Thursday morning because the woman who worked in their record department would get the new *Billboard* magazine in that day each week. I couldn't afford to buy it, so I'd ask her where "Shakin' All Over" was on the singles chart that week, and she'd say it was like #61 with a bullet. I'd still be going off to classes at the Manitoba Institute of Technology (now Red River Community College) to study business administration every day while our record was climbing the U.S. charts. We were so naive that we had no idea what having a single on the American charts meant.

It was early June and I was in my last year studying business administration, with final exams only a few weeks away, when the band got a call from an agent in New York. Our manager at the time, Bob Burns, had hooked us up with an agent there named Paul Cantor. Paul dangled the biggest carrot of all in front of us: He said he could get us on *The Ed Sullivan Show*. Elvis, Buddy Holly, and the Beatles had played the *Sullivan* show, and it was the biggest variety show on television. Everyone watched it on Sunday evenings. So Paul wanted us to travel to New York; all we had to do was get ourselves there. "Shakin' All Over" had become a hit in the U.S. The big time awaited us.

So there I was, cleaning out my locker at school, when the head of the business faculty came up and asked me what I was doing. I told him I was quitting because I was going to be on *The Ed Sullivan Show*. I'll always remember his reply: "You'll be back." He walked away shaking his head.

Paul Cantor managed Dionne Warwick, so he was a big-time player. However, he wasn't exactly straight with us. When he'd mentioned *The Ed Sullivan Show* he neglected to add the word "maybe." Nevertheless, the five of us drove non-stop, arriving in New York on Sunday evening when the *Sullivan* show was on. We made our way to the Ed Sullivan Theater on Broadway (currently the home of *Late Night with David Letterman*) and knocked on the back door. "We're the Guess Who. We drove down all the way from Canada. We're on the show tonight."

The guy looked us up and down, then checked his clipboard and replied, "Not this week," and closed the door. We later learned that what Paul Cantor meant was that if our record went Top 10 he could maybe get us a shot on the show. Our hearts sank.

All we knew about New York back in Winnipeg was a television cops and robbers show called *The Naked City*. So we were scared to death because we thought somebody got murdered every week in New York according to that TV show. We would only go from our hotel to Scepter studios and back. But after time went by and nobody was killed, we started venturing out further. We checked out Greenwich Village, Carnegie Hall, and the Empire State Building.

Florence Greenberg owned Scepter Records. She was a successful songwriter herself; she'd written "Soldier Boy" for the Shirelles. Actually, we thought Scepter Records was Spector Records, so we were going over the moon with excitement thinking we were going to be produced by the one and only Phil Spector. That's how green we were. When we arrived at Scepter Records to get our royalty cheque for "Shakin' All Over," it was $400 for the entire band. We'd sold a quarter of a million copies in the States and that's all we earned. We were ripped off, but that's the way it was for everyone back then. We didn't care. We were in New York!

Florence brought in music publishers who came to pitch songs for us to record. One of the songs we cut was Mitch Murray's "I'll Keep Coming Back." He had previously written hits for Gerry and the Pacemakers. We were also offered Artie Wayne's "Use Your Imagination," and two songwriters named Gary Geld and Peter Udell came to the studio and played us "Hurting Each Other." We recorded both songs. "Hurting Each Other" later became a big hit for the Carpenters. We also recorded Bruce Johnston's "Don't Be Scared." Bruce later joined the Beach Boys. We ended up recording quite a few tracks in New York that summer.

One day I was going up in the elevator to the studio and I saw two guys in leather coats and jeans. I recognized them right away. They were Burt Bacharach and Hal David, who were coming in to present their latest batch of songs to Dionne Warwick. I was hoping they would offer us some of their songs.

Instead, Florence brought in these three black high-school kids named Nick Ashford, Valerie Simpson, and Josie Armstead. They sat down at the piano and sang their songs for us. I think Florence was trying to turn us into an R&B soul group. We liked their stuff, and picked "Hey Ho (What You Do to Me)" to record. The three of them sang on the track with us and also did the backing chorus on "Hurting Each Other." Ashford and Simpson later wrote "Ain't No Mountain High Enough."

Florence's son Stanley Greenberg was the studio engineer and he was blind. That really blew us away. He knew the board by feel, so at first we didn't realize he was blind because he knew what he was doing. The studio had four tracks, meaning that we'd been moving up, track by track, from mono in Winnipeg to three tracks at Kay Bank studio in Minneapolis (where we recorded many of our early singles) and now to four.

After recording at Scepter Studios for a week, we went out on tour with the Kingsmen, working up and down the East Coast as far south as Florida. We were certainly wide-eyed, innocent Canadian prairie kids. It was the biggest thing we had ever done. The package tour included us, Dion and the Belmonts, and the Turtles. Sam the Sham and the Pharaohs did some dates with us, as well as Eddie Hodge, who had "I'm Gonna Knock on Your Door." Barbara Mason did some shows with us too, but she was so young her mother had to accompany her. We would do a fifteen-minute set: "Shakin' All Over" and a couple of other songs that nobody knew. They only recognized our hit, so sometimes we would open and close with it.

We were living one of those rock 'n' roll movies. We were away from home the entire summer and into the fall, living out of suitcases in and out of New York. The money was awful, but that wasn't the motivation for us. I don't know how we managed to survive. At every stop we'd get a room with two double beds and a cot, and share. We never knew when it would end, but we didn't want it to end. We were able to ride that song for the better part of a year because it continued to break out in different regions and kept getting airplay.

Back in New York, Paul Cantor asked us if we'd back up the Shirelles and the Crystals. We were good at copying records, so we said sure, and we did that for a few months. We would do our own set, take a break, then come out and back one of these girl groups playing all their hits, five white kids from Canada backing a trio of black girls.

But we had no idea we were walking into the 1965 race riots. We played places where there was blood on the floor. We drove through Georgia and saw the ghettoes. That was quite an eye-opener. We would go to gas stations with everyone in the same vehicle and guys would greet us with shotguns. We were called all sorts of horrible names for being with blacks. It was scary. We didn't know any better. When we played in Chicago there was a riot going on right in front of us on the floor, black and white kids fighting. It was unbelievable. We didn't have these kinds of problems in Canada.

I was amazed travelling with the Guess Who down South in the U.S. It was my first time in the rural South, and you'd be driving down the highway and look out and see these fields that were all white. They were filled with cotton plants. We got out and felt the plants, and they were just like the cotton batten we used back in Canada.

Once Scepter had enough tracks from our recording sessions, they released an album. But because it was primarily a black label, they put a black couple dancing on the cover and didn't include a picture of us on it. One of our first gigs in the States was at a black high school in Washington, D.C. We drove down from New York, but as we got to the gate everyone was staring at us. We were booked to play an after-school sock hop. The principal came up and asked us what we were doing there. "We're the Guess Who." And he replied, "No, you're not." So we had to show him the Canadian album cover and he eventually let us in, but it was a very weird experience.

### BURTON LORNE CUMMINGS

Following our U.S. touring schedule, keyboard player Bob Ashley left the group because he didn't like being on the road so much. One time the Crystals dragged Bob out onstage and stuck a leather jacket on him for "He's a Rebel." He was a real shy kind of guy and felt humiliated by that. Chad played piano for a while, but we needed a permanent replacement.

The Deverons were a North End Winnipeg band from St. John's High School that featured Burton Cummings on sax, piano, and vocals. They were all still in their teens and already a popular act throughout the city. Burton had made a name for himself after dancing on the grand piano at the Gerry and the Pacemakers concert at the Winnipeg Arena earlier that year. So when the Guess Who needed a new keyboard player we poached Burton Cummings from the Deverons. He was seventeen when we approached him, and still living with his mother and grand-mother. But he had the goods. He didn't hesitate. We called him in to Bob Burns's office and made him the offer. He made a joke about turning us down for an offer from the Beatles and then walked out the door, only to poke his head back in and ask, "Are you guys serious?" His life would never be the same; nor would mine.

Burton and I became buddies. His mother asked me to look after him because he didn't have a father, so I'd drive him home after gigs and pick him up the next day. I was like his big brother. But he had his own way of doing things and a rebellious streak, so he started to rebel against me. He didn't need a big brother anymore.

### LONDON CALLING

When our record "His Girl" on the King label made the British record charts we were giddy with excitement. Bob Burns had been contacted by Phillip Solomon at King Records, and we were invited to go to London, our dream come true. It was February 20, 1967, and a typical snowy Winnipeg day, but we had a big send-off at Winnipeg airport, with all the TV and press covering our departure. Many of our contemporaries on the local music scene showed up to bid us good luck because we were living their dreams. Naively, we thought we'd actually see Cliff Richard standing on a street corner or the Shadows and Beatles playing at the London Palladium. This was our Mecca. We couldn't wait to go over.

We borrowed money for airfare, fancy new stage clothes from the Stag Shop, and new equipment from Garnet, all totally financed. It cost a fortune to ship the gear over, but we figured we were about to hit the big time. The streets of London were paved with gold. We went expecting to become the new Beatles, but we were rewarded with being the new nothings. We had no contracts, no bookings, zilch. All that money spent for nothing. It left us $25,000 in debt.

We met some very undesirable and disreputable people there who tried to con us into signing a management and recording contract with them. On our first day in London, we went to the offices of King Records run by Phillip Solomon. He laid out his plan for us, which was no different from what most young, hungry, naive bands were offered in those days. The difference was that we'd already been through the mill with Scepter Records, so we were wary. It was a very one-sided contract that gave us nothing and gave them everything. They would put us on a weekly salary of £400 for the whole band. If we had hit records or toured, we'd still get the same salary and nothing more. I found out later that Van Morrison's band, Them, were signed to one of Solomon's contracts and never made a penny. It was presented to us as "Take it or leave it." I looked at Jim Kale, who was doing a slow burn. We all knew without even discussing it what our response would be.

"We'll leave it."

We got up and walked out. They thought they had us by dangling a British tour before our eyes. When we hit the street we looked at each other and realized, "What have we just done? We have no tour, no label, no money. Nothing." Bob Burns had failed to secure any contracts before we left. Our management team hadn't gotten anything in writing before we flew off to England. Our only saving grace was that we had return-trip tickets.

So there we were in London with nothing, jobless in the U.K. We had nothing to do—and yet we still had a wonderful time. We pooled all our money, which wasn't much, and rented one room at the Regent Palace Hotel in Piccadilly Circus. "Here we are in London, guys, let's make the most of it." Since we had our return tickets, we knew we'd get home. So we walked around and saw as many bands as we could in all the clubs. It was an incredible time. Probably the best two weeks of my life up to that point.

It was the custom in English hotels to serve a full breakfast—bacon, sausages, eggs, kippers, toast, cereal, muffins, everything—so we befriended the Spanish maids who pushed the breakfast trolleys from room to room. When the morning serving was over they would bring the leftovers to us. We literally lived on cold bacon and toast, which we made into bacon sandwiches, for the two weeks we stayed there.

I had a subway map, and each day I'd venture out around London, walking, riding the tube, and observing London life. I went to Carnaby Street and Soho and checked out record shops. I just figured that I may never be in London again. I soaked up all the sights and sounds of the city and would return to the hotel each night exhausted and have a bacon sandwich.

Walking around Soho, we met other songwriters. We met a guy named Reginald Dwight, who later changed his name to Elton John. We met a Canadian songwriter named Ralph Murphy from Ottawa who is still my very good mate today. We had on these Canadian pins because people had told us before we left that we wouldn't want to be identified as Yanks. They didn't like Americans over there. So we had these pins on, and Ralph saw us, and we kind of latched onto each other. He took us to his publisher, Mills Music, who had coincidentally published "Shakin' All Over," which had made a lot of money for them and Johnny Kidd's widow.

At Mills Music, the head of A&R, Tony Hiller, offered us a deal. If we would play for nothing on some demo sessions at Regent Sound Studios for other songwriters, he'd let us keep the tapes as our recordings. There was no money involved. It was just time in the studio. He also said we could record a couple of our own songs. We didn't have anything else to do, so we agreed. I quickly wrote a song for the sessions, "There's No Getting Away from You," in kind of a Walker Brothers style that I credited to Spencer Charles. We'd brought the first Buffalo Springfield album with us, so we recorded Neil Young's "Flying on the Ground Is Wrong." I'm pretty sure ours was the first cover of a Neil Young song.

After the two weeks, we came home to Winnipeg with our tails between our legs. We kind of snuck back into town and tried to avoid the humiliation of explaining what had happened, which was basically that nothing had happened. The one thing we had to boast about was that we had recorded in London.

Our other saving grace was that we brought back the latest sounds from the U.K. by groups like Cream and Jimi Hendrix. I took the first Hendrix record up to Doc Steen at CKRC and told him that this was what was happening over in England. He listened to it and then told me, "I can't play this on radio." But we brought 1967 England to Winnipeg. We started playing this wild psychedelic stuff around the city and smashing our equipment like the Who. People thought we had lost our minds. Initially, audiences didn't like the music, but within a few weeks they were coming back to hear it again. We had smoke bombs going off, and I would ram my guitar through a fake Garnet speaker cabinet that our road manager, Russell Gillies, would re-cover the next day. The kids never knew because it all looked brand new when we started the night.

Gar Gillies, Russell's dad, owned Garnet Amplifiers in Winnipeg and built me a special pre-amp unit so that I could get all the distorted Hendrix and Clapton sounds. I named it the

Herzog, and I'd put it on full blast so that it would make howling feedback noises. Gar also made me a custom whammy bar for my guitar that was longer than the normal ones, like a propeller, and that allowed me to do the Hendrix sounds. The Herzog became my sound, the sound of "No Time" and "American Woman." Over the years many guitar players have asked me how they could get a Herzog for themselves.

Soon deejays were hyping us on the air and there was a buzz going around about our new sound. "They're back from England! Come hear their new English sound!" We went from a few hundred curious people a night to thousands trying to get into the tiny little halls to see our incredible show. We were hip again because, just as years before in the Silvertones and Reflections, we were ahead of the pack in having access to English music before it hit these shores. Burton backcombed his hair like Hendrix, I had my Herzog and my whammy bar on my guitar sustaining and bending feedback notes, and all of a sudden we were heavy. Winnipeg had yet to witness any psychedelic music. Once again we were the trendsetters.

### LET'S GO

Faced with an enormous debt from our U.K. trip, we got an offer to serve as the house band on the weekly CBC-TV after-school television show *Music Hop*. With the Guess Who as backing band and our former lead singer Chad Allan as host, the Winnipeg edition of the cross-Canada series was renamed *Let's Go*.

Before we got the CBC gig, the show's producer, Larry Brown, asked if we could read music. The routine was that each week the show's musical director, Bob McMullin, wrote out the music charts for the musicians to play. Bluffing, I said, "Yes, of course!" Garry Peterson and Burton Cummings could read music, but Jim Kale and I couldn't. As a band we learned everything by ear from records. That's the way every band did it. A few days before our scheduled audition, I called Bob McMullin and asked him how he was progressing with the charts. He was nice enough to tell me both the titles he'd finished and not yet finished. So now that I knew the songs we had to play, I promptly went out and bought the records and called a band rehearsal, and we learned all the songs by ear. Two days later, when the music charts were placed in front of us at the CBC audition, we smiled at each other and began to play them. Not only did we play the songs perfectly, we sounded exactly like the records. Larry Brown came up to us and told us we had the gig.

It was hard work those two years. We even played the entire Beatles' *Sgt. Pepper* album in one episode. But the $1100 per week pay went directly towards our debt from London, and in the end, every penny was paid back. There was another great benefit from doing the show, though.

At the start of the second season, Larry Brown approached Burton and me with a proposal. "This is the perfect opportunity for you guys to perform some original material. Why don't you write some songs, and if I like them, I'll let you do them on the show." That's all the encouragement we needed. Burton and I would work at the piano in Burton's front room, putting our ideas together to create songs. At two in the afternoon Granny Kirkpatrick would bring us cookies and 7-Up, and we'd be done by four. A few hours later I'd swing by and pick him up for the gig that night.

Those Saturday songwriting sessions were something we both looked forward to, getting together with scraps of songs. It was the excitement of creating our own music that spurred us on. We both wanted to be songwriters like Brian Wilson, Jagger and Richards, Bacharach and David, or Lennon and McCartney. Even with the differences in our personalities, we still connected. There was just a chemistry that happened, and the result was some great music. I became McCartney to Burton's Lennon, the missing piece to his puzzle and he to mine. I'd bring a nearly completed song to him and he'd play me one of his song fragments. Then we'd take the strengths of each and piece together a completed song. From that came the Bachman-Cummings songwriting team.

### GO NORTH, YOUNG MEN

We did a northern tour of Canadian air force bases in early 1968 that was sponsored by the Department of National Defence and broadcast live to remote communities above the 60th parallel. We thought it would be a cool experience, and the money was good, so we agreed to go along. We were booked to perform alongside Ted Komar and his orchestra. Ted played accordion, and the other players were well-established local jazz musicians. Headlining the tour was CBC singer and ex-Winnipegger Juliette, star of her own long-running television series. Her show followed *Hockey Night in Canada* for decades. A magician and a comedian rounded out the troupe. We were the token pop act.

We were told to wear our warmest clothes. It was the middle of winter, forty below in Winnipeg, and we were heading north towards the Arctic Circle. I had this cool sheepskin coat that was bulky but warm, and we all wore scarves, toques, mitts, and boots. When we showed up wrapped up in our winter wear these air force guys proceeded to give us even more clothes to put on, telling us, "Where you're going you'll need these extra clothes." As big as my feet are, size thirteen with big winter boots on, they put them into another pair of sheepskin-lined boots with galvanized rubber on the outside. With six pounds on each foot, I could barely walk. They then gave us parkas to be worn on top of our parkas. As he was handing me mine, the officer told me, "By the way, the buttons are made of compressed, dehydrated soup, and inside the hood is aluminum lining. If you take it out, put some snow in it, and place it in the sun, you can heat up the buttons and eat the soup. In your pocket is some Sterno and matches to start a fire." This coat was a walking survival kit. I thought to myself, "What have we gotten ourselves into?!"

We boarded an air force cargo plane called an Atlas, the kind where the entire front end lifts open and trucks drive right on in. In the middle of the fuselage they had a couple of rows of theatre seats bolted to the floor. It was freezing onboard, so we were glad to have the extra warmth of the survival coats.

Our first stop was Churchill on Hudson Bay, then we headed off to places like Inuvik beyond the Arctic Circle. For the crowds, seeing Juliette live, watching a magician make rabbits disappear, and listening to a real live rock band that appeared on television was a real treat. The whole community would come out to the shows—old, young, Moms and Dads, Native and non-Native.

The guys in Ted Komar's band were real partiers. They were being paid well and the music was a breeze to play, so they were drinking pretty good. It soon turned into high school hijinks all over again. One night at another one of these remote outposts somewhere, Juliette was onstage performing, backed up by the Komar band guys who were half smashed. Burton decided to have some fun. He proceeded to make this huge cardboard sign three feet wide. On one side he printed "Applause" and on the other he put "F... You." In the midst of one of Juliette's numbers, he strolled right across the stage between her and the musicians. The crowd saw "Applause" and erupted. Juliette was all smiles because she figured it was for her. She couldn't see Burton. Meanwhile, the band cracked up and fell over in hysterics because they saw the other side of the sign. The music momentarily fell apart as these guys cut up. Juliette turned around to see what was happening to her accompaniment, but by then Burton was already offstage. When we completed the tour, the Canadian Armed Forces gave each of us a plaque showing a map of the North and little flags where we'd stopped.

## THE MARVIN POLANSKI TAPES

I've served as unofficial archivist for the Guess Who, releasing our early recordings, including the group's first three Quality

Records albums and a double CD compilation entitled *This Time Long Ago.* Over the two years the group appeared on CBC-TV's *Let's Go,* only two of the shows had been preserved on videotape. A lot of musical history was lost, including some of the earliest attempts at songwriting by Burton and me.

Marvin Polanski, who worked on the show, had been in my grade 12 class at Garden City Collegiate. Years later I was being interviewed for Bravo TV's Lenny Breau documentary and Marvin was the sound man. He said, "Do you remember me?" and I said, "Yeah!" He had replaced the sound man on the *Let's Go* show back in the late 60s.

So as I'm doing this interview outside at the Forks in Winnipeg, Marvin says to me, "I was so proud to be working on that show because I knew you and Garry Peterson from school."

I'm going, "Yeah, that's cool," but I'm trying to do the interview, so I'm not paying much attention to him.

Then he says to me, "And I saved all the tapes from the show." Now he had my undivided attention.

CBC would erase the tapes each week and reuse them to save money, but Marvin had dubbed audio copies of the shows on reel-to-reel tapes and still had them some thirty years later.

"Can you go home and find them and send them to me?"

A few weeks later I received a box full of tapes, and when I played them I couldn't believe I was listening to this stuff for the first time in decades. It was amazing to be hearing ourselves at that early stage in our career. We sounded so innocent. It's incredible that this stuff wasn't lost forever. The tapes became the *Let's Go* album, with us doing cover tunes like "Along Comes Mary" and "White Room" plus some of our early attempts at "These Eyes," "No Time," "Minstrel Boy," and "When You Touch Me."

## BRAVE BELT

In May of 1970, as "American Woman" sat at #1 in *Billboard,* I left the Guess Who and returned home to Winnipeg. The four of us had grown apart as people, as bandmates, and as friends, and we had different lifestyles. I didn't party, do drugs, smoke, or drink; they all did. I needed to be home with my family for a while. But I wasn't done with music.

Between my departure from the Guess Who and the launching of Bachman-Turner Overdrive in late 1972, I put together Brave Belt. With me were Chad Allan, Fred Turner, and my brothers Robbie and Tim. Managing the group was my older brother Gary. The band's sound was aimed at the growing country rock scene, but it was clear early on that the country rock thing just wasn't working for us. Still, although a commercial failure, Brave Belt was an important transition for me from the Guess Who to BTO.

People still expected Randy Bachman to be rockin', not Crosby, Stills and Nash or Poco. We had done the first Brave Belt album, but it bombed, so I was looking to retool the engine. I knew we needed a harder sound and that Fred Turner's voice was perfect for that. Unfortunately Chad Allan wasn't onside with this and left the band. So we were now the Bachman brothers and a Turner.

We still had some bookings as a country rock band, and one of them was at the Saddledome in Calgary with Ferlin Husky and Canada's country music "Traveling Man," CBC-TV's Tommy Hunter. We all used to watch *The Tommy Hunter Show*. At the Saddledome, Brave Belt was the closing act after these country music legends. The crowd was a country music crowd. In our earlier incarnation we'd have gone down a lot better, but we were now BTO in everything but name.

So we played our set, and when the lights came up at the end there was no one left in the arena. We'd emptied the place. Everyone had walked out on us. The next day the newspaper had rave reviews about all the other acts, but for us it had two lines at the bottom that said: "At the end of the show, four Vikings from Winnipeg came out and blew everybody's face off." The promoter refused to pay us. We couldn't check out of our hotel because we had no money. Later that day we ran into Tommy Hunter in the hotel lobby. He told us that what had been done to us was wrong and that he was organizing the other acts to go on strike against this particular promoter unless he paid us. "It's not your fault the promoter made a mistake booking you guys." Thank you, Tommy. In the end we got paid.

We ran Brave Belt on a shoestring budget. We had little money and often had to travel huge distances to play for only a couple of hundred dollars. I paid each of the guys a salary out of my Guess Who royalties. If I hadn't done that, we wouldn't have had a band. Often we had to travel way out west somewhere on a weekend, come home again, then go out west again the following weekend. It was becoming too expensive driving back home only to head out again a few days later. As well, I'd be flying out during the week to pitch our third Brave Belt album, which ultimately became *BTO I,* to record labels across the U.S. The other guys couldn't afford to stay in hotels during the week, so they tented.

My dad had a tent we used to take on camping trips as kids, so Robbie and I knew how to camp. The band would drive to Calgary, look for a suitable site to pitch the tent, do the gig, and return to the tent for the night, making sure no one was following us to discover our impoverished existence. We had a Coleman stove, and we'd bring a loaf of peanut butter and jelly sandwiches from home. Or we'd cook up some soup. I remember coming back from a trip to Los Angeles trying to sell *Brave Belt III* and finding the tent covered in frost and snow, Robbie and Fred huddled together inside trying to keep warm.

Our battered old Econoline van was like a sieve on the highway. It had holes and cracks where the wind would whistle in. The heater and defroster couldn't keep the windows clear of frost or fog. When it was forty below outside, it was forty below inside. So we had a big leather glove-like cover for the front of the van to keep the draft out and some of the heat from the engine in. My father-in-law, Bob Stevenson, would make us large Sterno cans from empty Empress Jam pails. They had a roll of toilet paper soaked in alcohol with a wick in the middle, and we'd put two of them on our dash to keep the windows clear and a couple on the floor to keep our feet from freezing. We would travel back and forth across western Canada like this in the dead of winter, sometimes all the way to Vancouver and back with these burning cans of alcohol all over the van. Hardly the glamorous life of a rock star! But what these experiences did was foster a strong bond between us. It was an "All for one and one for all" spirit. I called it Brave Belt Boot Camp, and it really helped us cope when the big success as BTO finally came.

With Brave Belt we were trying to be like Neil Young and the Buffalo Springfield or Poco and do a cool kind of country rock like that. It was clear that it wasn't working, though. People were confused as to what I was trying to do, and maybe I was confused, too. But with Chad Allan's departure, Fred Turner stepped up as our lead singer, and overnight we had a different sound. Fred had what I used to call this Harley Davidson voice, gritty and strong, very similar to John Fogerty in Creedence Clearwater Revival. Having a different lead singer, a guy with a more powerful voice, I found I could write different songs, more powerful songs. And so we evolved from a mellow country rock band into playing pretty cool rock 'n' roll. We played a lot of Stones, Who, and Creedence in our live shows. They all had that primal rock 'n' roll beat. That's where our sound came from.

We were clearly not Brave Belt anymore. We'd had two albums out as Brave Belt, and it was time to change our name because we weren't that band. My record label kept telling me, "You've got to put your name, the Bachman name, in the band so that people will recognize the guy who wrote all those Guess Who songs. The radio stations will recognize your name and you might get some airplay." From their perspective it made perfect sense. Why try to hide my identity? My brothers Rob and now Tim were in the band, so we had three Bachmans and a Turner, and for about two weeks we called ourselves Bachman Turner. This was the era of acts like Brewer & Shipley, who were playing acoustic folk–style music, and Seals & Crofts, who played acoustic guitar and mandolin. We were playing this heavy-duty rock 'n' roll.

But when promoters would hear the name Bachman Turner, they thought it was two guys with acoustic guitars playing folk songs like Seals & Crofts or Brewer & Shipley. So we got booked into these coffee houses with little tables. We'd come in and set up our big amplifiers and blow the cups off the tables and get fired. We needed a name that showed clearly that we played heavy music, not "Diamond Girl" or "One Toke Over the Line."

We were coming back from a gig in Windsor, Ontario, one night, and we drove across the border to Detroit. We stopped at a gas station, and as I was paying I looked right by the cash register and saw a magazine called *Overdrive*. I called Fred over and said, "Look at this magazine! It's all about trucks!" It even had a centrefold, but when we opened it out, it was a picture of the inside of a guy's truck cab with leopard-skin seat covers, a stereo, and a little rack to put a book on—these guys actually read pocketbooks as they're driving these semi-trailers! I said to Fred, "This is a great name for an album," and he replied, "This is a great name for a band!" No longer would people think we were a folk duo. It was a name that left no doubt we were a heavy-duty band: Bachman-Turner Overdrive.

I called the record label the next day because they'd been bugging me to get a name that had my name in it. They liked it but said that it was too long for people to remember, that we needed a one- or two-syllable name like Byrds or Beatles, something like that. So I said, "Well, there's the initials BTO …" They thought that was fabulous. So we got the name to go with our sound.

### THE RADISSON AND GROSEILLIERS OF ROCK 'N' ROLL
During the time of glam rock and platform boots, BTO weren't wimps or pretty boys. We looked like mountain men in furs, fringe, flannel, and long beards. We were the Radisson and

Groseilliers of rock, two hearty voyageurs who lived in the woods and never shaved. We were perceived by some as the lumberjack rockers from Canada who'd blow the windshield out of your car. The media picked up on that rustic image and really ran with it. Fred was a big guy like myself and had this flaming orange hair and beard. He even had a coonskin hat and these big, fringed jackets with beads. Fred looked like Mike Fink, King of the Keelboaters, right out of Davy Crockett. We were rugged men from the northern wilds of Canada. We'd come out on stage and the music was full-tilt stomping with Fred screaming at the top of his lungs over sledgehammer guitars and drums that sounded like falling trees. So our image matched the sound coming out on the records. We were a "Tim Allen's Tool Time" guy's band. Guys loved BTO. I remember on our whole tour of the U.K. we didn't see one woman at the shows. We appealed to the ordinary Joe kind of guy.

We dressed like Neil Young: farmers' flannel or denim shirts, jeans with patches, lumberjack boots. The difference was that while Neil looked frail with a twenty-eight-inch waist, we were size thirty-eight, soon to become forty-eight. He was a young tree while we were mighty oaks. The legend that surrounded us in the early days, and I remember actually reading this in a magazine, was that we were lumberjacks living in the forest who found guitars abandoned in an old car. We didn't eat a peanut butter sandwich, we ate a loaf of peanut butter sandwiches. We didn't eat a piece of apple pie, we ate the whole pie. We didn't live in houses, we slept outdoors in the snow.

### *My Picks*

"AIN'T NO MOUNTAIN HIGH ENOUGH" by Ashford and Simpson

"DUNROBINS GONE" by Brave Belt

"FLYING ON THE GROUND IS WRONG" by the Buffalo Springfield

"FLYING ON THE GROUND IS WRONG" by the Guess Who

"HEY HO (WHAT YOU DO TO ME)" by the Guess Who
(with Ashford and Simpson)

"HIS GIRL" by the Guess Who

"HURTING EACH OTHER" by the Guess Who
(with Ashford and Simpson)

"JUST LIKE ROMEO AND JULIET" by the Reflections

"LIGHT MY FIRE" (Jose Feliciano version) by the Guess Who

"LIGHT MY FIRE" (the Doors version) by the Guess Who

"NEVER COMIN' HOME" by Brave Belt

"SLEDGEHAMMER" by BTO

"THIS TIME LONG AGO" by the Guess Who

# Lenny, Neil, and Me

The two musicians who've had the most direct and enduring impact on my life and my career are Lenny Breau and Neil Young. I came in contact with both growing up in Winnipeg, and both continue to inspire me.

## LENNY BREAU

Jazz guitarist extraordinaire Lenny Breau mentored me in my early years learning guitar, and his lessons remain at the core of my own style of playing. Lenny was the ultimate technician of the guitar, incorporating elements of classical, flamenco, rockabilly, and jazz into a unique approach that few others have been able to master. There was only one Lenny Breau.

He was born in Auburn, Maine, and moved to Winnipeg as a teenager. He was only a few years older than me. Lenny started playing guitar at age seven and left school at age ten. There was no point in him continuing at school. All he wanted to do was play guitar, and so his parents, Hal and Betty Breau, let him quit. By the time he was twelve, he was playing full time in his parents' band, the Lone Pine and Betty Cody Show, and travelling. Lenny was truly a music guy. He could barely read or write. He couldn't even balance his cheque book. But he would practise his guitar fifteen to sixteen hours a day. He just played guitar all day because he wanted to master it all.

In the late 50s Lenny was touring the Prairie provinces, playing shows with his parents. In the middle of their sets they would say, "And now we're going to turn it over to Junior, who's going to play you a song. Take it away, Junior!" Junior was Lone Pine Jr., and when he'd take over it sounded like a whole band playing. I could hear bass and chords and a melody all at the same time. I thought Junior was a band.

Once at the end of their show, Lone Pine announced that next week they'd be playing live in the car lot at Gelhorn Motors on North Main across from Kildonan Park in West Kildonan. That wasn't very far from where I lived, so the following Saturday I hopped on my bicycle and rode over to Gelhorn Motors to see what Junior was, because I loved the music. I'm watching the band and Lone Pine and Betty perform when Pine says that they're going to take a break and turn it over to Junior. I'm waiting to see this little combo come out, and instead this little guy steps forward and starts playing all by himself. He's really young, about my age, very slight and fragile looking, sporting dapper clothes and a string bow-tie, with hair well groomed and a pencil-thin d'Artagnan moustache. He was playing the most beautiful guitar I'd ever seen, an orange Gretsch Chet Atkins model 6120 almost bigger than him. And as he's playing, I'm hearing bass lines and chords plus a melody lead line, but he's doing it all by himself. That was my introduction to Lenny Breau. That day he played "Caravan" and covered all the parts simultaneously by himself. I thought it was the most amazing thing I'd ever seen or heard.

Afterwards, as the band was packing up, I approached Junior.

"Can I ask you something?" I said.

"Sure, man," Lenny replied in this hushed, hipster-sounding voice.

I asked him what that style of playing he did was called. I was still a beginner, but I'd had years of violin so I had the finger dexterity.

"It's called Chet Atkins," Lenny replied.

I thought it was one big word, like flamenco. Chedatkins. I'd never heard of Chet Atkins and thought it was just a particular style of playing. Nonetheless, I wanted to learn it. He told me to get a "chedatkins" record and get that style into my head first before I could learn it.

"Go to Eaton's record bar and ask for a Chet Atkins record," Lenny directed me.

So one day after school the next week, I took the bus down to Eaton's department store on Portage Avenue and said to the woman at the record bar, "I need a 'chedatkins' record."

"You mean Chet Atkins?"

"No. Chedatkins. It's a kind of guitar style, like flamenco."

She grinned at me and replied, "I think you mean Mr. Chet Atkins. He's a guitar player."

She went behind the counter, pulled out an album, said "Listen to this," and put it on. "That's Chet Atkins."

So I bought the record, took it home, and learned "The Third Man Theme" all by myself, figuring out first the bass line and then the melody and putting them together.

A couple of weeks later, the CKY Caravan played another car lot in the North End. After their set, I approached Lenny again. He recognized me, so I asked him if I could come over to his house sometime and learn a few things from him. To my eternal good fortune, Lenny had moved across the street from two schoolmates of mine, the Schmolinger twins, Carol and Karen, on Airlies Street in the North End. What was further cool about Lenny was that even though he was still a teenager, barely sixteen, he didn't go to school. The guitar was his life. That's what I wanted to do, quit school and play guitar all day.

I went to school the following Monday morning, but at lunch

I made my way to the Schmolingers' house. After lunch as they returned to school, I went over and knocked on Lenny's door. He was in his bedroom with his guitar and a record player. I showed him what I had worked out, "The Third Man Theme," and he showed me what I was doing wrong because I didn't know the proper chords.

From that moment on I was the hunger and Lenny was the nourishment. I visited his house many times over the next couple of years. Everything I wanted to learn I would struggle at and then have Lenny show me what I couldn't get. He would show me the simpler way of playing it. And he had an incredible ear. Lenny could literally hear something once and play it, invert it, solo over it, everything. No formal lessons, just Lenny and me in his bedroom with a guitar. I have no tapes, no notes, no pictures of him and me together, only my memories of this gentle, soft-spoken young man sitting in his bedroom showing me where to move my fingers. It was probably the greatest couple of years of my life in terms of my learning curve, and it gave me the foundation for my playing style today because I started integrating those ideas and styles into my stage playing soon after.

I blew a lot of time and a couple of years of high school because I wanted to play Chet Atkins–style guitar and later rock 'n' roll, and Lenny was teaching me. He was developing his own style of playing, a combination of lead on top, the chords in the middle, and a walking bass line all at the same time, as well as mastering harmonics and clusters of chords. When I put a Lenny Breau record on today I get the same feeling I had the first time I ever heard him on the radio as a teenager: One guy alone can't be playing all those parts.

Lenny moved to Toronto and became a great jazz player, the greatest ever. From time to time I'd run into him. I'd be telling him about our success in the Guess Who, and he'd reply in that hipster whisper of his, "Yeah, man, that's cool, but are you playing any jazz? You gotta do a jazz thing, man." Lenny went on to become a true guitar genius. Guitar players would travel thousands of miles to see him play and beg for a lesson. All I'd had to do was knock on his door.

After Lenny's tragic death in 1984 I began thinking about the debt I owed him for what he did for me and my career. I remembered his words, "You gotta do a jazz thing, man." But while rock 'n' roll was always way easier for me, jazz was frightening. It had all these weird notes in it. I could play all those rock 'n' roll songs with one hand tied behind my back, but I had fenced myself in. Jazz was like jumping over that fence and going out into the world and finding out what it's like to do something different. It was a huge, gigantic step for me to make a jazz album, but by the new millennium I was ready to take that leap. There was an element of danger for me, an artistic danger. I was a rock 'n' roll guy. I could fall on my face. But it was good for me to be challenged, and attempting to play jazz was certainly a challenge for me.

For years, fans, friends, and other guitar players had been telling me to do an entire album like "Undun" or "Looking Out for #1," but I never felt confident enough. Once I made up my mind to do it, though, I took some jazz guitar lessons and practised for several years to be able to tackle that style of playing and its musical language. I wanted to be conversant in that language, and so I immersed myself in it. I didn't have the jazz vocabulary and had to learn it. I would use one lick from Tal Farlow one night and another from Barney Kessel the next night and Lenny Breau the next and integrate these into my own playing style.

I didn't want to do a lot of instrumentals because that's what people would be expecting from me. I did an instrumental album, *Axe*, back in 1970 and it sold maybe twelve copies. Now I wanted to write jazz songs. I wanted to write a new jazz standard. I think "Our Leaves Are Green Again" is that kind of a song. I wrote it with Stephan Moccio, who's written songs for Celine Dion and Josh Groban. I worked real hard for three years in between

Guess Who reunion tours, getting jazz musicians together and writing these songs with some of the best songwriters. I think my instincts were right.

I also tackled reinterpreting some songs on the album. One in particular came from my earliest experiences on guitar. The first three chords I ever learned were the chords to Johnny Cash's "I Walk the Line" on my cousins' big Gibson guitar. The song is really a love song, but he never says "I love you" anywhere in the lyrics. It's got no chorus, no bridge; every verse just ends with "Because you're mine, I walk the line," saying that to his woman. It's very moving. I wanted to arrange it in a jazz style. I was fooling around with that song one day, and when I tried it in minor chords it sounded even more haunting and beautiful. I really like the way it came out on the album.

One of the thrills for me on *JazzThing* was getting to do a duet with Lenny. We never recorded together when he was alive, but through the magic of digital technology we were able to play together. I had some candles lit in the studio, and I'd found a song that I felt I could comfortably sit in on called "Breau's Place." It felt just like jamming with him live. I also did the Gershwin standard "Summertime" with Lenny on tape. I made it as though we were in the studio together; I trade my vocals with his guitar and I scat with him and against him. The experience was almost seance-like. I could certainly feel his presence. When it came time to title the album a year later, I just figured I'd call it *JazzThing* because Lenny would always tell me I needed to do a jazz thing.

### NEIL YOUNG

In the fall of 1960, not long after my informal lessons at Lenny Breau's house, fifteen-year-old Neil Young moved to the south end of Winnipeg from Toronto. His mother, Rassy Raglan, was a celebrity on a local TV show called *Twenty Questions*, and my mother idolized her because she had a job and my mom was just a housewife. Neil formed his first band, the Jades, a few months after arriving in town. He later played in the Classics and the Esquires before he formed the Squires in 1963. That's when I became aware of him. Neil used to watch me playing up onstage, and afterwards he'd wait around to ask me questions about things he'd seen me do on guitar. He was already writing and recording his own material. Like me, Neil developed an appreciation for Hank Marvin and the Shadows sound and even purchased an orange Gretsch 6120 Chet Atkins model guitar like I had. Neil's distinctive guitar style is less about the technical virtuosity and more about the fire and intensity he brings to the instrument.

The Squires recorded Neil's first session at radio station CKRC in 1963, with deejay Bob Bradburn producing and Harry Taylor engineering. It was an instrumental called "The Sultan" backed with "Aurora." The following year they cut Neil's first vocal recording, a song he wrote called "I Wonder." Afterwards he asked Harry Taylor what he thought and Harry replied, "You're a good guitar player, kid, but you'll never make it as a singer."

The first song Neil sang in public was at Kelvin High School in the cafeteria in early 1964. There was no microphone, but his manager, and my friend, Lorne Saifer, knew that the Shaarey Zedek synagogue nearby on Wellington Crescent had one. There was a banquet or something being held that night and a microphone had been set up at the head table. So Lorne and Neil "borrowed" it. Lorne says today that Neil "blessed" that microphone.

I remember playing a dance at River Heights Community Club in the south end and being introduced to Neil Young. Lorne introduced us. Neil was a skinny, dark-haired kid who stood to the right of the stage, my side, and watched me all night. I'd heard of him because in Winnipeg you tended to know of other guitar players who were good. I'd run into him later at the Paddlewheel restaurant at the Bay where all the musicians hung out or at Winnipeg Piano checking out the guitars.

Neil had ambition. Community clubs weren't enough for him. He was already writing his own songs. Other than us, most bands in the city weren't doing that yet. He had a dream and nothing was going to stop him from fulfilling it. When he left Winnipeg most people laughed at him. "We'll never hear from him again."

But, of course, we did hear from Neil Young. After trying his luck in Thunder Bay and Toronto, Neil headed to Los Angeles. In a Sunset Strip traffic jam in April 1966, he met up with Stephen Stills and Richie Furay, and together with Bruce Palmer and Dewey Martin, two Canadians, formed the Buffalo Springfield. With three singer/songwriters in one band, they were an instant sensation in the clubs on Sunset Strip. The Springfield was one of my favourite bands. Although they were together only two years and released only three albums, their legacy remains impressive.

Neil Young came back to Winnipeg in December 1966 to visit his mother, and while there he invited our band down to CKRC to play us the first Buffalo Springfield album. I remember Burton and I were kind of jealous. Neil had left Winnipeg and made it, and he was singing his own songs on the album. The Springfield was the coolest group around. We absolutely loved them.

"You won't believe this," I remember Neil telling us at CKRC. "It's recorded on eight tracks. You can record guitar after guitar." We were in awe. We had only ever recorded on three or four tracks. As we were listening, we got to one track in particular.

"Who is that singing?" I asked.

"It's me," he replied. "It's like Bob Dylan. People really don't care what it sounds like. If you've got a really weird voice, somebody out there will like it as long as you deliver it with honesty."

I've never forgotten that. Neil took a lot of negative comments about his voice, even back in Winnipeg, but he was never deterred.

Neil and I don't have great singing voices like Burton Cummings or the Springfield's Richie Furay, but our voices are distinctive.

The Guess Who learned that first Buffalo Springfield album inside out. We played "For What It's Worth" in our shows as well as "Flying on the Ground Is Wrong," which we thought was a real gem from Neil. We later recorded it. When their second album, *Buffalo Springfield Again,* was released in 1967, on the back cover each of the guys in the band listed their influences. It was a big dedication, and when I got the album, boy, was I surprised to see my name among that list. It was an unbelievable thrill for me to be included with the Beatles, the Kingston Trio, Hank Marvin, Otis Redding, Ricky Nelson, the Ventures, Eric Clapton, Phil Spector, and so on. Neil had spelled my name "Backman" but that didn't matter. It was still me.

Neil returned to Winnipeg again in January 1971 to play two solo acoustic shows at the Centennial Concert Hall on his "Journey Through the Past" tour. I was there for one of the shows and backstage afterwards. I had just formed Brave Belt with Chad Allan, and we'd recorded our first album but didn't yet have a record contract. Backstage, I told Neil the name of the band and he thought it was cool. I played him some cuts from the album the next day, and he liked it. When I told him we didn't have a record label, he told me to go see Mo Ostin at Reprise Records in L.A., which was Neil's label.

I did go to L.A. and play Mo Ostin the test pressing of the Brave Belt album, and he offered me a deal. I think they called Neil to verify who I was and if I was legit. That night I went with one of the Reprise Records people to see Neil give a fabulous show at the Dorothy Chandler Pavilion. I couldn't for the life of me imagine that this kid who'd been at Kelvin High School just a few short years earlier was now onstage in Los Angeles, alone without a band. To my amazement, the audience sang every word to every song. Neil was their darling. I just sat there stunned and enchanted by this kid I used to know in Winnipeg, the kid who'd left town in an old hearse and who'd made a big splash in Los Angeles.

After that I didn't see Neil for a long time. In June 1987 we shared a stage together for the first time ever at the Winnipeg Convention Centre for the "Shakin' All Over: Bands and Fans Reunion," playing "American Woman," "Takin' Care of Business," Bob Dylan's "Just Like Tom Thumb's Blues," and "Down by the River." That was a special night for me. But we didn't get much time to talk or hang out.

Then in 1993, Neil's guitar tech and roadie, Larry Cragg, got in touch with me. He was looking for a couple of Gretsch switch tips for Neil's Gretsch guitars. Switch tips are the ends of the toggle switches guitars have to change from one pickup to another, thus changing the tone of the guitar. The tip can fall off after a lot of use and you just screw it back onto the switch. If you put a little nail polish on them when you screw them in, they stay longer. Being the "Gretsch Guru" and owner of hundreds of Gretsch models, I did have some tips, so I faxed Larry back telling him I'd send him a few. In the package I also put in a copy of the lyrics to a new song I'd written about growing up in Winnipeg called "Prairie Town." I had no other intention but to show it to Larry Cragg, whom I'd known for a long time. Amazingly enough, the next day a fax came through for me saying, "Hi Randy. I love the lyrics to 'Prairie Town.' I'd like to be part of this song. Call me. Love, Neil."

In the lyrics I talk about things like learning to drive in the snow, freezing at the corner of Portage and Main, how I grew up on one side of Winnipeg and Neil on the other side, Neil and the Squires playing the Zone, which was the Twilight Zone club on St. Mary's Road he used to play at all the time. So Neil invited me down to his ranch, Broken Arrow, just outside San Francisco. I told him I had a slow and a fast version of the song, acoustic country and electric rock. That's something he'd done with songs like "Tonight's the Night," "Hey Hey, My My" and "Rockin' in the Free World." He said he wanted to play on both versions, and so we did the slow version and the fast version of "Prairie Town."

When I came home I was so thrilled to have Neil Young on my solo album that I sent a copy of the song to my attorney, Graham Henderson, who had secured the deal for me with Sony Music in Toronto. The next night my phone rang and it was Graham, and he said, "Listen to this." Over the phone I heard "Prairie Town" with me and Neil singing. But between our two voices I heard a female voice. Graham was married to Margo Timmins, singer with the Cowboy Junkies. Graham was playing my tape and Margo was singing live in the kitchen. "She doesn't know I'm calling you and letting you listen," he said. So I told him to please interrupt her and ask her if she'd like to come out and sing on the track. I was mixing it in two days. She flew out to Vancouver and added her voice to the track. Her beautifully ethereal voice is like the sweet icing on the cake.

Years later, when I was visiting Neil's ranch to record "Spring Is Nearly Here," a song we recorded together for a Shadows tribute album, I told him about a song I'd written called "Made in Canada," a real grungy guitar rocker. We were sitting at the dinner table and Neil said, "Why don't we record it right now?" He's a spontaneous guy, so I seized the moment and replied, "Great! Let's do it!" My son Tal was with me on drums and Richard Cochrane on bass. We recorded it in a barn with farm animals roaming around outside. In fact, before the take, the recording engineer had to go outside and shoo away the goats and chickens so we wouldn't pick them up on the tape.

I ran through the song, showing Neil the chords. It's pretty simple. We did it one more time and then Neil said, "Okay, let's go." As we got to the end of the song where he was supposed to solo, he became transfixed, like he was in a trance. His hair fell over his face as he kept going on and on soloing like a maniac.

The three of us just kept following him. He was soloing with wild abandon, as he does in his song "Like a Hurricane" with Crazy Horse and the wind from a giant fan is trying to blow him over. It was incredible. He went from a double to a triple solo, stomping on his big red foot-pedal board as the sound suddenly swirled and swooped around us. He kept going: eight, nine, ten solos. It was like playing with Jimi Hendrix. Then suddenly it was over.

"That's it. We got it. Good night, guys."

I'd thought we were just doing a run-through, but he'd had his engineer rolling the tape. He always has the tape rolling to capture the moment. "Made in Canada" appeared on my 1996 solo album *Merge*. Recording "Made in Canada" was an incredible experience.

## My Picks

"AURORA" by Neil Young and the Squires

"BREAU'S PLACE" by Randy Bachman and Lenny Breau

"I WALK THE LINE" by Randy Bachman

"LOOKING OUT FOR #1" by BTO

"MADE IN CANADA" by Randy Bachman and Neil Young

"OUT OF MY HEAD" by the Buffalo Springfield (featuring Neil Young)

"PRAIRIE TOWN" (fast version) by Randy Bachman and Neil Young

"PRAIRIE TOWN" (slow version) by Randy Bachman,
Neil Young, and Margo Timmins

"SUGAR MOUNTAIN" by Neil Young

"THIRD MAN THEME" by Chet Atkins

"UNDUN" by the Guess Who

## Lenny Breau CDs for Further Listening

*Boy Wonder* (Guitarchives)

*Chance Meeting* (Guitarchives)

*Cabin Fever* (Guitarchives)

*Live at Bourbon St.* (Guitarchives)

*Live at Donte's* (String Jazz)

*Pickin' Cotton* (Guitarchives)

*The Hallmark Sessions* (Art of Life Records)

## *Randy's 10 Favourite Neil Young Songs*

1. "Southern Man"—This song really captures a northerner's impressions of the Old South and its prejudices and traditions. The lyrics are great and the guitar solo rips part of your heart out with its angst and attitude.
2. "Like a Hurricane"—Again another combination of great lyrics and soulful guitar playing. The video for this has Neil trying to stand up against a powerful windstorm, and that's kind of symbolic of his career.
3. "Sugar Mountain"—I love the simplicity of the silly lyrics and the childlike chorus that anyone can sing along to.
4. "Down by the River"—The lyrics tell it like it is and the guitar solo breathes in and out of different attacks on the strings.
5. "Heart of Gold"—A different, more casual, folky Neil with a cool blend of acoustic guitar and harmonica.
6. "Mr. Soul"—Great lyrics and a guitar riff like the Stones' "Satisfaction." (I'm amazed Keith Richards never sued over that.)
7. "Only Love Can Break Your Heart"—Again, a different Neil, this time playing piano with a great sing-along chorus. His versatility amazes me.
8. "Expecting to Fly"—Neil doing another switcheroo with a Beatlesque mix of tempos, textured with an array of different instruments, sound effects, and lyrics. Impressive every time I hear it.
9. "I Am a Child"—Just a great easy melody with lyrics seemingly written by a child or the child inside Neil.
10. "Rockin' in the Free World"—The title says it all. It's wild, frantic, urgent, and everything a great rock song should be.

# The Story Behind the Song, Part 1

In 2002 I put together a tour concept called "Every Song Tells a Story" where I would share with audiences the stories behind the songs I'm best known for from the Guess Who and Bachman-Turner Overdrive. At each show the audience was enthralled by the stories and sang along to the songs. The tour was a tremendous success and led to a live CD, a concert DVD, and a songbook. People seemed to really like the intimate, insider background stories to the songs. I've shared a lot of them on *Vinyl Tap* over the years.

### "TRIBUTE TO BUDDY HOLLY"

In 1962 Chad Allan and the Reflections cut our first record, a 45. It's a cover of a song we heard from England by Mike Berry and the Outlaws about Buddy Holly's 1959 plane crash. I remember some friends of mine and I were going to drive down for Buddy Holly's show in Fargo when we heard the news that morning that his plane had crashed.

We recorded the song in Minneapolis at Kay Bank studios. We'd bought the Trashmen's record "Surfin' Bird," and on the label it said

"Recorded at Kay Bank Studios, Minneapolis." Winnipeg lacked a decent studio. CKY and CKRC had recording studios, but the best you could get was mono or two-track recording. So we phoned down to Kay Bank and inquired about their studio. They offered three-track recording. "Wow, one more track!" So we pooled our money and booked a couple of dates over a weekend in late 1962. My girlfriend Claudia Senton's dad worked at Birchwood Motors and he loaned us a Buick to use. I borrowed my uncle Jack's little box trailer for the equipment. We used to go on tenting trips as a family, so I asked my dad if we could borrow his canvas tent. We set up the tent in the trailer, put the equipment inside it, and collapsed the tent over it all with a couple of bricks on top to keep it from blowing away. And off we went to Minneapolis.

At the studio session, Chad Allan had a sore throat and wasn't feeling well. And my Gretsch guitar wouldn't work. There was something broken in the wiring, so I had to use Chad's new Fender Jazzmaster electric guitar while he strummed my Gretsch acoustically. His Jazzmaster had a thinner sound because it had a solid body, so I wasn't happy with the sound I got. But we managed to record four or five tracks. We signed with Canadian American Records and released our first single, "Tribute to Buddy Holly." By the time we released it, we were Chad Allan and the Reflections. What an amazing moment for me when I heard that record and my guitar playing on the radio for the first time. We thought that was the big time for us.

Between 1962 and 1964 we recorded further singles at Kay Bank and released them on the REO and Quality Records labels. They all charted in Winnipeg and the Prairies, but none had a national impact until "Shakin' All Over."

### "SHAKIN' ALL OVER"

Recorded under very minimal conditions in the middle of a chilly Winnipeg winter night at a local television studio, "Shakin' All

Over" was the song that catapulted us to national success and gave us our name, the Guess Who. "Shakin' All Over" was released in January 1965 and represents the thriving 1960s Winnipeg community club dance scene. Imagine the movie *That Thing You Do* multiplied by a thousand, and that's what the 60s Winnipeg music scene was like.

Chad Allan had a friend named Wayne Russell who had an amazing record collection from overseas. He also had all these reel-to-reel tapes of the British hit parade. As a Christmas present each year, his cousin in England would tape her favourite 45s and send them to him. Or she'd tape British radio and send him those tapes. As I mentioned earlier, for rock 'n' roll–crazed kids like us, it was like discovering buried treasure. These were songs we never ever heard in Winnipeg. We used to learn the songs right off the tapes, sometimes without knowing the title of the song. That's how we learned "Till We Kissed" and found out much later that the title was actually "Where Have You Been All My Life." And that's how we first heard the Beatles in early 1963, a full year before their records hit over here. In amongst Wayne's collection we found "Shakin' All Over," a hit in Britain for Johnny Kidd and the Pirates back in 1960 that never crossed the Atlantic. That song just leapt off the tape at us. The guitar riff still turns heads forty years later. We loved the song immediately and wanted to record it.

We were friends with a guy named Bob Burns who hosted an *American Bandstand* clone show in Winnipeg called *Teen Dance Party,* which was recorded live at CJAY TV studio at Polo Park every Saturday afternoon at two. Kids would dance to the latest hit records that Bob would spin, and they'd have a local band on from time to time. I remember Neil Young telling me he'd gone to *Teen Dance Party* because his girlfriend at the time was a dancer with the Pepsi Pack, but that he didn't go on the show because he didn't know how to dance or was too self-conscious. We played the TV show a couple of times when we were the Expressions.

So one time, it was in late December 1964, we convinced Bob to let us into the CJAY TV Channel 7 building late one night so we could record there. It was too cold and too expensive for us to travel to Kay Bank studios in Minneapolis. We'd played a community club gig that evening, and so it was the middle of the night when we got to the station. We bribed the janitor a few bucks and paid a recording engineer to come in. We set up our gear in the middle of this empty studio where they hosted *Teen Dance Party*. For the TV show they had this big black velvet curtain to hide all the wires and technical stuff. So we pulled that around us to deaden the sound. In the middle we had one microphone, the one Bob used to announce the records he would play. We set up around this one mike and recorded our songs. Jim Kale had a Fender Concert amp that all the instruments were plugged into. No separation at all: my lead guitar, Chad's rhythm guitar, Jim Kale's bass, and a contact microphone stuck on the back of Bob Ashley's piano. We did one take of "Shakin' All Over," and when we listened back, the drums were too loud. So we went back to the studio floor and moved Garry Peterson's whole drum kit a couple of feet back from the one microphone.

We did several takes before we got the sound right. It was just a monophonic one-channel tape recorder, so when we'd come up to the booth to hear the take, the engineer had to patch the cords from record to playback. This happened several times. We'd record, put our instruments down, and go up to the booth to listen to the playback. But on this one take the engineer forgot to patch the cords back, and what we heard was the same sound Elvis used to get on his early Sun records: a slapback echo. That was the sound we wanted, and that became the take we kept. It became the sound of "Shakin' All Over."

When we sent the tape in to George Struth at Quality Records, he decided to simply credit the group as "Guess Who" so that radio programmers would give the song a spin. Canadian recordings didn't get much airplay in those days, so George knew he needed to trick programmers into playing the record. The deception worked. "Shakin' All Over" became a national hit under our new name, the Guess Who. It was Top 10 or better right across Canada. Following up a hit, though, is always difficult. You're only as good as your latest record, and while our subsequent releases did well in Canada, none matched "Shakin' All Over" in excitement and appeal.

### "HIS GIRL"

In 1966 Burton Cummings joined the Guess Who and, soon afterwards, Chad Allan left. He had problems with his throat and he had problems with Burton. They didn't get along. That meant Burton was the lead singer now. We were given a song to record by Whitey Haines, the head of BMI in Canada, who told us it was going to be a hit. We'd been touring one-horse towns in Saskatchewan all summer for $400 a night but had little money left by the end of the summer to pay for a recording session. So I took what money I had and went to the horse-racing track and won enough to pay for a session. Off we went to Minneapolis to cut "His Girl," written by Canadian songwriter Johnny Cowell. "His Girl" marked a change in our usual choice of singles because it was a sweet, soft ballad and we were a rockin' band.

We brought along Gar Gillies and his trombone. Gar was a well-known big-band trombone player who we knew because he made our amplifiers for us. It started out with me getting Gar, who owned an appliance store, to fix my amplifiers when I'd blow them out. We were playing larger and larger venues, and our Fender amplifiers just couldn't cut it. So Gar started souping up my Fender amp before making amps for us. This was the start of Garnet Amplifiers, which became the sound of the Guess Who, BTO, and the sound of Winnipeg.

Gar played the trombone solo in the middle of "His Girl." The record was a hit across Canada in the fall of 1966. In early

1967 it was licensed to King Records in the U.K. They took our three-track tape and sweetened the recording by adding strings, glockenspiel, and additional guitar. That became the first Winnipeg record to make it onto the U.K. record charts. At the end of the song, Burton Cummings does his little Sam Cooke thing like from the end of "You Send Me," that "Oh la ta ta ta ta ta ta a a."

When "His Girl" made it into the U.K. Top 50 we thought we were going to be stars. In our minds, as I said earlier, the streets of London were paved with gold. We borrowed a ton of money, bought all new gear and travel cases, all new stage clothes, and flew everything to London only to discover we had no contracts and bookings. It was a disaster. But we survived and "His Girl" became a Top 20 hit across Canada, marking another important step in our progress from local cover band to international recording artists.

### "THIS TIME LONG AGO"

We took a huge gamble flying off to London in February 1967. We expected a big welcome at the London airport. Instead there was nothing, not even any contracts for us. It was a costly mistake, but we did manage to record four songs with producer Tony Hiller. Tony worked for Mills Music, which had made a lot of money off our recording of "Shakin' All Over." He came to our hotel, where we laid out our dire situation, and he offered us an opportunity to cut some demos for him.

Tony took us to Regent Sound Studios in Soho to record two Mills Music songs written by British songwriters Jimmy Stewart and Jerome Langley, "This Time Long Ago" and "Miss Felicity Grey," which we thought were pretty decent. While we were recording at Regent Sound, I happened to look up at the acoustic tiles on the walls and spotted a little pattern where the dots had been punched out, creating a funny little caricature of a person. I followed the dots and at the bottom was a signature: J. Lennon. I asked the studio engineer if the Beatles had ever recorded there, since they usually recorded at Abbey Road studios, and he told me they were indeed once there recording some demos. So I asked him if I could have the tiles, but because they were tongue and groove, I'd have had to take the whole wall. Still, it was pretty cool recording where the Beatles had once been.

We recorded over two days, just before we had to go home. We laid down the tracks on the first day and the overdubbing the next. We were nervous being in a London studio, but as soon as the engineer counted down the track, we just did our thing very professionally. Tony Hiller thought we were great. We were already better than the average British band because of our years of experience. Cy Payne, the arranger, wrote a score for flugelhorn and added glockenspiel and a few other things to improve the tracks. Despite our initial dislike of the flugelhorn, it made the record sound like the Fortunes, a British Invasion band.

Tony took the tapes to Fontana Records, who worked out a licensing deal with Quality Records back in Canada to release them in the U.K. The singles did nothing over there, but "This Time Long Ago" became a hit for us that summer back in Canada. The tracks we cut in London with Tony served as the all-important transition from the derivative sound of our previous recordings to a more professional and original sound. Tony Hiller has since become a very good friend of mine and I see him whenever I'm in London.

### "PRETTY BLUE EYES"

This was the worst record of all time by the Guess Who, trust me. We'd recorded some songs in England that we thought were pretty good, so we wanted to break our contract with Quality Records Canada and sign with someone else bigger. We thought we'd record a song originally done by Steve Lawrence called "Pretty Blue Eyes" and do it really, really badly. Our plan was to send Quality something that was so bad they'd say to us, "We're never going to release this and you're off the label." So we went into Gar Gillies's Garnet Amplifiers shop on Ferry Road in the St. James suburb of Winnipeg. Gar made all our amplifiers for us.

Gar had an old Robertson tape recorder with two inputs and we had a couple of mikes. To make it sound really bad we had Burton sing through a trumpet bell so that it sounded like a megaphone, and instead of a bass drum we had a Coke bottle and someone blowing into it going "Whoooo." It was like a jug band. We had a real cowbell in there and guys moooing. For the cymbals Gary used an electric drill that went *Rrreeeeerrrr! Rrreeeeerrr!* So it sounded like *Boom Boom Rrreeeeerrr!* Burton Cummings did his best Walter Brennan impersonation from *The Real McCoys* TV show and those old cowboy movies. We recorded it with this crazy stuff, and the middle is just a train wreck with all these noises and Gar Gillies playing trombone.

This was the Guess Who trying to get out of our recording contract. So we recorded it and prepared to send the tape to Quality Records. But we didn't have any money in case they decided to sue us, so we had second thoughts about sending it in. We chickened out. So we recorded a good version without all the nonsense and sent both to them. They liked the good version and released it with the bad version on the B-side, and it made the charts across Canada. In the end we failed to break our contract with Quality Records.

### "THESE EYES"

The record that changed it all for us was, of course, "These Eyes." I wrote the piano part for "These Eyes" in Regina one night waiting to take Lorayne Stevenson, my future wife, on a date. That was back in the summer of 1966 and we hadn't known each other long. She wasn't ready, so as I waited and noodled around on her parents' piano in the living room, I came up with the chords. I'm not a piano player, but I sat down at the piano and I started playing these two chords, Dm7 to Cmaj7. I liked how they sounded and decided I would write a song with those chords. The words I had were actually "These arms" with the line "These arms long to hold you."

Burton Cummings and I used to meet every Saturday morning at his grandmother's house, Granny Kirkpatrick, on Bannerman Avenue in the North End of Winnipeg to write songs. We each kept these Hilroy notebooks with us all week and would jot down any ideas for songs we came up with. Then we'd show each other what we had and see if we could come up with a song. So Burton listened to my two chords and my words to "These Arms." I also had the descending progression down to the A minor chord. He said, "Hmmm. Can we move that to the second line and make the first line 'These eyes cry every night for you'?" Then we came up with "These arms long to hold you again." He also had the long line "These eyes have seen a lot of loves but I'm never gonna see another love like I had with you." It all fit together perfectly. And from that we wrote a song that would forever change our lives. "These Eyes" started out with a guy who could only play piano in the key of C, and that's why the beginning is so simple. That's all I could play on the piano.

In 1968 we took a demo of that song to Jack Richardson, the man who would become our record producer, in Toronto. He later took us to New York to record at A&R Studios with the great Phil Ramone and engineer Dave Greene. They didn't want the intro to be played on a full piano. They wanted something different, so Burton played it on his little Hohner electric piano which had a built-in tremolo. That became the opening and the signature sound of "These Eyes."

Jack bought out our contract with Quality Records in Canada and signed us to RCA Records in New York. We actually didn't want "These Eyes" to be our first single with RCA. We saw ourselves as a rock 'n' roll band, not a smooth ballads band. We wanted a rocker like "When You Touch Me" as our first single off *Wheatfield Soul*. RCA and Jack Richardson wanted "These Eyes," and they won. Jack sat us all down and told us, "This is the best song on the album. You have no other chance. I've mortgaged my house for this." He was right. RCA paid less than $10,000 for the *Wheatfield Soul* album with "These Eyes" on it. Don Burkhimer at RCA Records told me years later they would have paid ten times that because they believed in "These Eyes" being a hit. It became our first million-seller.

### "LAUGHING"

After "These Eyes" became a huge hit, we still wanted to release a rocking song. Don Burkhimer at RCA instead pressured us for another soft pop song. He took us out to a New York deli and told us, "Just give us one more like 'These Eyes' and you'll never have to work again the rest of your lives."

Soon after that, in early 1969, I remember we were sitting on our tour bus waiting for the ferry to Vancouver Island. I really liked the opening minor chord strumming of the Bee Gees' "New York Mining Disaster 1941," but instead of a minor chord I turned it into a major chord and just started playing the opening chord. We took the chord progression from the Dave Clark Five's "Because," which was a fairly standard chord pattern used in lots of songs. Burton even used it later in "Stand Tall." Then we added the background vocals pattern from the old Platters song "Twilight Time," the ascending "ah's," and put them in behind the lyrics. This was all done right on the spot sitting on the bus. That got us started. The rest of it was original, the idea of laughing at someone who broke your heart. We both loved Roy Orbison's hit song "Crying" and thought the idea of laughing was clever. We also liked the buildup in "Crying" where it starts quiet then builds to a crescendo. "Laughing" was finished in about thirty minutes. It was one of those songs written to order and gave us our second gold record. Sometimes songs can come so easily.

## "UNDUN"

It was in late 1968 and we'd been touring with Frank Zappa and the Mothers of Invention and Alice Cooper. We'd played a date together in San Francisco and were in Vancouver for another show. It was Saturday morning and I was sitting around in my hotel room listening to CKLG FM radio. FM radio was still fairly new and very adventurous. There were no formats; they played whatever they wanted, including long album tracks, jazz, blues, you name it. I'd been carrying these jazz chords around in my head for months. Burton Cummings and I had tried doing something with them, but we couldn't come up with anything. We couldn't think of any lyrics that fit. So I'm listening to CKLG when the deejay played Bob Dylan's "Ballad in Plain D," and somewhere in all the lyrics Dylan sings, "She's come undone." That was the spark I needed.

I immediately turned off the radio and started writing out lyrics to these jazz chords I'd had for months. I wrote all these verses, ten or twelve, and I played it later for Burton. He said, "Wow, that's great. Pick three verses and we'll record it." We put it on the flip side of our second single, "Laughing," and when that song began slipping from the charts some deejay flipped it over and "Undun" became a double-sided hit, pushing the single over the million-selling mark.

We actually re-recorded "Laughing" and "Undun" without RCA's approval. According to our contract with them, we were required to record in their own studios. So we recorded our second album, *Canned Wheat*, with "Laughing" and "Undun" on it at their New York studio, but it was an old place and the technology was outdated. It had giant studios with high ceilings for orchestras. But for drums the sound was awful. Garry Peterson would hit his drum, and all you'd hear was a tinny little click rather than a solid thump. No matter how much we tried, we couldn't get a sound we liked. Because *Wheatfield Soul* had been an independent production we could go wherever we wanted, and so we'd cut it at A&R Studios in New York. Although the sound we'd gotten was fantastic, RCA wouldn't let us go back there. So now we had ten days to record *Canned Wheat,* and we weren't happy with the sound. We'd already tried "Laughing" and "Undun" and didn't like it at all. We wanted to go back to A&R Studios with Phil Ramone to do the album.

So Jack Richardson secretly booked us into A&R for a late-night session. We paid for it ourselves. We went in, laid down two songs, "Laughing" and "Undun," then went back to RCA studios and pretended to be recording. Then we said, "We're done the album." You can tell when you listen to those two songs on *Canned Wheat* that they stand out in terms of sound from the other tracks. When RCA found out about our clandestine recording there was nothing they could do about it because it was too late. The album was completed. But they heard the obvious difference in the two tracks. You can still hear it. That's why those two songs are so good.

"Undun" gave the Guess Who that rarest of accomplishments: a double-sided hit single. Not a lot of recording artist have achieved that. But we were still pegged as a soft pop band and we wanted to rock.

### "NO TIME"

In 1967 Neil Young's band, the Buffalo Springfield, released their second album, *Buffalo Springfield Again.* Burton Cummings and I took that album and listened to it over and over, dissecting the music. As songwriters, that's what you do and what we did. You listen to what others are doing and you're influenced by that. We kind of wanted to do country rock like the Buffalo Springfield. They were one of the first bands doing that and they were great. The Guess Who started out as a rockin' band, although our first single, "These Eyes," was a ballad. But we still wanted to rock and have a rock hit record. We wanted a Buffalo Springfield kind of song.

There was a cut on the second Springfield album called "Hung Upside Down" with a great guitar riff that Stephen Stills played. So I took that riff, turned it around, and came up with the intro riff to "No Time." When we were in San Francisco, the whole Haight-Ashbury scene was happening. Besides all the hippies and flower power, we saw guys who looked like they wanted to run away from the States and come to Canada. These were peace-loving guys who didn't want to be sent over to Vietnam. We overheard some of them talking, and one guy said to another, "Where have you been? I haven't seen you for a while." And the other guy replied, "I've been to the killing floor," which was a term used in slaughterhouses or abattoirs. We heard that phrase over and over, and finally we asked someone what it meant and they told us it was slang for the Vietnam War, being sent to the killing floor. Burton Cummings and I put that in our song "No Time." "No time for a gentle rain, no time for my watch and chain. No time for revolving doors, no time for the killing floor." Basically it meant no time for the Vietnam War. This was before we cut "American Woman."

Burton and I wrote that song together, and we liked it so much we not only included it on our second album but re-recorded it and put it on our third album, *American Woman*. "No Time" became a million-selling single for us in early 1970. What's interesting is that Mike Post, who writes television theme songs, uses the same chord progression from "No Time" in the theme for the TV show *Law & Order*. So I hear that ten times a night on television. "No Time" bridged the gap for us, and we followed that with "American Woman." That single and the album both went to #1.

### "AMERICAN WOMAN"

I remember we were booked to play a gig in Kitchener, Ontario, in the late summer of 1969. But it wasn't a concert like the ones we were doing in those days, with just one set. This was a dance like in the old days, where we'd play three sets of dance music.

We were excited because we could play our Beatles, Doors, and Animals songs. So we'd been onstage for a while when I broke a guitar string on my Les Paul. In those days I didn't have a spare guitar or a guitar tech to change it for me. I had to do it myself. So I said to the guys, "We have to take a break." The guys left the stage and I stayed there to change my string and tune it up. We would sometimes signal each other that the break was over by one of us going up onstage and starting to play the first song of the next set. We'd all recognize the number and come onstage to join the others. I started to play a chord pattern, "dum dum dadada dada dada dada dum dum dadada dada da dum," and Garry Peterson and Jim Kale came onstage and joined right in behind me on the riff. We were looking to jam a bit. I started to solo over their rhythm then went back to the riff again. We just kept going and going and really digging it.

Burton Cummings was outside the arena having a cigarette when someone said to him, "Aren't you playing with the band?" He looked up and didn't recognize the song, so he ran up onstage yelling to me.

"What are we doing?!"

I replied, "We're jamming in E. Play something."

Burton grabbed his harmonica and played a solo, then picked up his flute. Then he did a piano solo. I took another guitar solo. He came towards me onstage and I yelled to him, "Sing something!" As he stepped towards the microphone, the first words he uttered were "American woman, stay away from me." Right off the top of his head. He sang it maybe four times, I soloed again, he sang it again, and we ended the song.

The place went absolutely nuts. We figured we had something with this jam, but we weren't sure what it was quite yet. It wasn't a song that Burton and I had sat down and written with verses and chorus. It was just a jam riff. We played it again at other gigs after that and it got better and better as we played it. When we went into the studio a few weeks later Burton strung together lines like "war machines and ghetto scenes," just rhyming words. I had part of the lead guitar line but didn't have the end. Burton had the final four-note riff for "New Mother Nature," that "da do do da" line, so I just borrowed that. When I tried it in the studio, everybody dug it. But we couldn't pull the song together in the studio because it had been just a jam and it didn't have its own tempo yet. It was all over the place, speeding up, slowing down, stopping and starting. I remember we had a whole frustrating day of working at it in the studio.

Garry Peterson and I went in the next day and I just plugged my Stratocaster into a Fender amp with tremolo. It had a much cleaner sound. That seemed to get the groove going. Then Jim Kale added bass and Garry added some East Indian tabla drums that Jack Richardson brought in. That became the basic backing track. I overdubbed another guitar doing the lead using my 1959 Gibson Les Paul and Garnet Herzog. Then Burton put the words on. "American Woman" was born onstage but completed in the studio.

People always tell me what a really heavy song it is, almost a heavy metal guitar riff. But it's really not that heavy. I'm not using a two hundred–watt Marshall stack and grinding out these heavy power chords. It's a fairly light rhythm track. It's the thickness of the lead guitar lick that gives it the heavy sound, and Burton's vocals sound like he's yelling in defiance, as if he really means it: "American woman, stay away from me."

The American woman we were singing about wasn't the average American girl on the street but the Statue of Liberty and that poster of Uncle Sam pointing and saying, "I want you!" So when that song became #1 we were labelled a protest band, but we were just a bunch of guys from the Canadian prairies.

A few months earlier we'd had a situation where U.S. authorities tried to draft us. We had green cards by then and were crossing the Manitoba–North Dakota border at Pembina. I remember the American customs guard telling us to pull in half a mile beyond the border under the sign saying Selective Service. Just before that sign was a gas station, and since American gas prices were cheaper than Canada's at the time, we always filled up in the States. We drove in to fill up and started talking to the attendant. I asked him where the Selective Service building was.

He looked at me and replied, "You don't want to go there." Then he told me that his son had been drafted and was fighting in Vietnam. "I suggest you turn around right now and go back up to Canada."

So we did that, and didn't dare try to cross the same way again. Part of that might have been the sentiment behind "American Woman." It was easier to say than "Uncle Sam stay away from me" or "Statue of Liberty stay away from me." It was all unplanned. RCA used that imagery, though, in their promotion of the record: the Statue of Liberty with the face of an old woman superimposed over a New York alleyway with trash everywhere. It was at the height of the Vietnam War, so the timing was perfect.

"American Woman" stayed at #1 for three weeks on the U.S. national charts in May 1970. That year we sold more singles than any other rock act, and we sold more records than the entire Canadian recording industry combined to that point. "American Woman" was recently voted the greatest Canadian single of all time. I'm not surprised.

### "NO SUGAR TONIGHT"

In early 1969, after playing a gig in San Francisco, I was in Berkeley, California, and had just bought a bunch of vinyl records. That's something I often did in different cities on tour. I'd be looking for unusual or hard-to-find albums. So I was taking these records back to my rental car when I saw three guys in black leather jackets walking towards me on the same side of the street. I was a little intimidated by this. They looked like guys from a biker gang, three rough, tough street guys and me, the lone Canadian. I'm six-foot-three but I certainly don't look threatening. Plus I'm a Canadian. I'm a lover, not a fighter.

As these guys walked along, people parted like waves, stepping aside to let them through. They were walking shoulder to shoulder and coming straight towards me. So I nonchalantly crossed over to the other side of the street, trying to avoid them, and they did the same, still bearing down on me. The three guys are getting closer and closer, giving me the eye. I could feel a confrontation coming.

Suddenly this battered little brown car pulls up in front of them. It's got dents in the front fender, a blue door, and the back window is all smashed like a spider's web held together by duct tape. This little woman steps out and starts yelling at one of these tough guys. The other two scatter; they don't want anything to do with this. She's ragging on this one guy who doesn't appear so tough now as he's standing there being chewed out by a tiny woman. He no longer looks menacing; he looks embarrassed by this woman tearing a strip off him.

"You're nothing but a no-good bum!" she's yelling. "You left me at home with the kids again. You're supposed to be looking for a job and here you are with your buddies checking out the girls."

So he sheepishly goes around to the passenger-side door.

Finally she says to him as he's getting in the car, "And baby, when you get home you ain't gettin' *no sugar tonight*."

I wrote "No Sugar Tonight" as part of a unique collaboration. It was our producer Jack Richardson's idea to combine my song with a Burton Cummings song, so we got "No Sugar Tonight/ New Mother Nature." But when it came time to pick a B-side for "American Woman," Jack chose to chop Burton's song off and release "No Sugar Tonight" as a separate track. When "American Woman" started sliding from the charts, deejays flipped it over to find another hit. The *Billboard* record book shows that "American Woman/No Sugar Tonight" are the longest and shortest songs (double A-sides) to reach #1 in the charts.

## *My Picks*

"HIS GIRL" by the Guess Who

"HUNG UPSIDE DOWN" by the Buffalo Springfield

"LAUGHING" by the Guess Who

"NO SUGAR TONIGHT" by the Guess Who

"NO TIME" by the Guess Who

"PRETTY BLUE EYES" (bad version) by the Guess Who

"PRETTY BLUE EYES" (good version) by the Guess Who

"SHAKIN' ALL OVER" by the Guess Who

"THESE EYES" by the Guess Who

"THIS TIME LONG AGO" by the Guess Who

"TRIBUTE TO BUDDY HOLLY" by Chad Allan and the Reflections

"UNDUN" by the Guess Who

# *Randy's Guitar Shoppe*

If there's one thing I know about, it's guitars. I have several hundred of them. Keith Richards is rumoured to have eighteen hundred guitars. Back in the early 60s the Winnipeg Piano Co. at the corner of Portage Avenue and Edmonton Street in downtown Winnipeg was a great place for guitars. On the main floor were the pianos, sheet music, and all that stuff. But when you descended the stairs to the basement, that's where they had all the electric guitars on the wall—brand-new Fenders, Gibsons, and Gretsches—and amplifiers on the floor. Guys like me, Fred Turner, Neil Young, and other local guitarists would stare at these beautiful guitars and dream of playing them. The sales clerks there were very supportive of young kids like me wanting to buy guitars. When Fred Turner was maybe fifteen years old he went to Winnipeg Piano and got a guitar and amplifier, but when his dad wouldn't co-sign the contract for the payments, the store clerk let him keep the stuff, telling him, "I think you'll play this. Just come in whenever you have a few dollars." If it hadn't been for that sales clerk, Fred likely would never have played guitar.

My first electric guitar was a Silvertone model from the Simpsons-Sears catalogue. It was $35, a lot of money for a teenager in the 1950s. I remember seeing a local band, I don't even recall their name, but the guitar player was Eugene Hywarren. I thought he was absolutely cool. He had flat-top hair with the sides slicked back and he was playing a cool-looking Harmony electric guitar. At that time I only had an acoustic guitar. So I went up to him and asked if I could come to his house and play his electric guitar, and he said sure. He later found me that Silvertone guitar. I still have it. It's funny, but the cheap guitars back in the early 60s— Silvertone, Harmony, Hagstrom, Supro, Danelectro, Kay—are much sought after today. These were the beginner guitars back then and are hard to find now. I guess everybody threw them out once they moved up to a better model. But these beginner guitars had their virtues.

I just loved the sound of an electric guitar. I would go to the country-and-western music shows at the old Winnipeg Auditorium and watch the guitar players. When *Bonanza* came on the television every Sunday night everything stopped at our house. We all watched it. For me, though, I loved the theme song played on electric guitar by Al Caiola. He had so much reverb on his guitar that it sounded as if he were playing in a cave or a tiled bathroom just to give it that depth and big sound. My dad would say that one guitar was the same as another, but I knew early on that different makes and models produced different sounds.

In the spring of 2008 I introduced one of our most popular themes with *Vinyl Tap* listeners. Over several weeks I featured profiles of the guitars that changed the sound of rock 'n' roll. There are three or four makes of guitars that every player knows should be in your guitar arsenal. They're like your tools: your hammer, your saw, your screwdriver. Most guitar players need a Fender Telecaster and a Fender Stratocaster, a Gibson hollow-body electric and a solid body, a Gretsch, and a Rickenbacker. In *Vinyl Tap*'s "Guitarology 101" we explored all these guitars—the sounds that made them unique and the recordings that were made using them.

## FENDER TELECASTER

Our first guitar is the Fender Telecaster. Some of the people who've played Telecasters for years are known as the Masters of the Telecasters. Some you know and some you don't. The Telecaster has a very bright, clean, trebly sound. But there's a thickness to it as well. The first time I ever heard a Telecaster sound was Luther Perkins backing up Johnny Cash in the Tennessee Two. It was in the first song I ever learned on guitar. My cousins, the Dupas brothers, had a guitar, and they taught me the three chords to "I Walk the Line." Once I learned those three chords I was on my way.

I later played with Johnny Cash in Brandon, Manitoba, way back when I was in the Silvertones with Chad Allan, before we became the Reflections (then the Expressions, then the Guess Who). It must have been about 1962. Johnny came out with these two guys, Luther Perkins on guitar and Marshall Grant on bass. When they'd first started with Johnny back in the 50s none of them knew much about playing their instruments, but Luther knew a bit more than the others, so he got to play lead guitar. His lead playing was so simple that it appealed to everybody and helped define Johnny Cash's sound. It was that LCD thing, the lowest common denominator.

The first Telecasters were called Broadcasters. There was also a single-pickup model with the same body called an Esquire that had the bridge pickup only.

When Fender issued its Broadcaster, Gretsch already had a guitar of that name, and Fred Gretsch sent Leo Fender a letter informing him that he couldn't use the name. So Leo changed the name to Telecaster. He didn't change the guitar, just the name. But nowadays an original Broadcaster, or better yet a "No-caster," which were the handful of models he made in between the name change, sell for big, big bucks.

Leo Fender started his company in 1947 making Hawaiian lap steel guitars. They made them out of a two-by-four with a pickup on it, and that gave them the idea to make a solid-body electric guitar. Fender claimed that they made the first solid-body guitar, but others were working on the same idea at the same time, so there are plenty of counterclaims as to who was really first. In evolving from making lap steel guitars to solid-body regular guitars they kept the back pickup, which had a bright sound to it because Hawaiian music required that bright sound. It made the Telecaster very trebly and bright, yet not tinny. But if you take a Telecaster and crank it through a loud amplifier, it has a very piercing sound.

The cool thing about a Telecaster is that you can throw it off the roof of your house, pick it up, and it'll still play because it's just a piece of wood. They can take a lot of abuse. The body is about a two-inch-thick slab of wood and the neck is bolted on with four bolts. So if you don't like the neck, you can just take it off and bolt another one on. I used to take the neck off my Telecaster and put the two pieces in a small suitcase for travelling, and then put it together to play a gig. Telecasters are probably the most durable and distinctive electric guitars. Best value for your money and one of the most enduring guitars ever. You can hear Telecasters played in rock, country, blues, jazz …

If you listen to Johnny Otis's 1957 record "Willie and the Hand Jive," it's got a great Telecaster sound. Another great Telecaster sound is on Gene Vincent and the Blue Caps' "Whole Lotta Lovin." The Blue Caps' lead guitarist, the great Cliff Gallup, switched from a hollow-body Gretsch to a Fender Telecaster after the band got an endorsement deal with Fender. When I saw them in Winnipeg back in the late 50s they had all new Fender amplifiers and guitars.

Dale Hawkins was born in Goldmine, Louisiana, and was Ronnie Hawkins's cousin. Dale recorded a song in the 50s called "Susie Q," and the guy playing that memorable lead line was James Burton, who went on to play with Ricky Nelson and Elvis Presley. James Burton became synonymous with the Fender Telecaster.

When Norman Petty, who owned Buddy Holly's song publishing, sold that catalogue to Paul McCartney's company, MPL, Petty threw out the old recording equipment that had been used to record those classic Buddy Holly and Fireballs recordings in Clovis, New Mexico. A friend of mine, Wes Dakus, happened to be there at the time, and he told me that all this old recording gear that still worked was piled up by the garbage. So I managed to get some of it, and I have it in my own studio. If you plug a Telecaster or a Stratocaster into the recording console like Buddy did, you get that distinctive sound he had.

Two of the original masters of the Telecaster were Roy Buchanan and Danny Gatton. These two guys could coax the most amazing sounds from a Telecaster: moans, howls, and screams. The great thing about a Telecaster is that even though you might play it through a distorted amp, you can still pick out every note distinctly. When you did crank up your Telecaster, it made this great growling sound.

Roy Buchanan played with Dale Hawkins after James Burton. Roy could squeeze the most amazing sounds from his old battered Tele. No pedals or effects. He made the guitar cry by using his volume pod. He spent some time up in Canada playing guitar for Ronnie Hawkins and the Hawks, and his understudy was a teenager named Robbie Robertson, who adopted Roy's Telecaster sound. After Robbie became the Hawks' lead guitarist every guitar player in Toronto had to have a Telecaster like he played.

By the late 50s everybody wanted that Telecaster sound in rock and rockabilly, and in country music as well with Buck Owens and Don Rich from the Buckaroos. In England there was an embargo after the war on a lot of U.S. goods, so guitar players over there couldn't get Fenders very easily. One of the first Telecasters in the U.K. was used on Johnny Kidd and the Pirates' "Shakin' All Over" in 1960. It was a clean Telecaster sound, but it was so powerful. Johnny Kidd's real name was Frederick Heath and the Pirates' guitar player was the legendary Mick Green. He was a big influence on a lot of U.K. guitarists, including the Who's Pete Townshend.

The first time I heard Booker T. and the MGs' "Green Onions" I was drawn to Steve Cropper's Telecaster sound. It almost sounds as if he's simply making a bunch of noises the way he played his Telecaster through a small amp with distortion. That sound changed my life the first time I heard it. It's not like he's playing a chord; he's just making a noise, but it's the coolest noise. Steve Cropper was another one of those Masters of the Telecaster. He asked Leo Fender to build him a Telecaster made out of solid rosewood. That was a heavy guitar to hold and it had a heavier sound. Leo Fender made two of these. The other one was sent to George Harrison of the Beatles. Now, I know that when people see the Beatles performing on TV or live, George is usually playing a Gretsch Country Gentleman or Tennessean or a Rickenbacker 360 twelve-string, but he used other guitars in the recording studio. Listen to his sound and tone on "Let It Be."

The second pickup they put on the Telecaster, farther up the body towards the neck, was the most useless thing ever. It was very bassy and nobody used it. The only player I ever saw using that second pickup was Canadian jazz guitarist Ed Bickert, who used it constantly. Everybody else just used the bridge pickup because it has such a bright sound.

The Yardbirds were a 60s British Invasion band who were much more than that. Their producer had them record pop songs to get their name out there, but basically they were a blues band. In the Yardbirds' history were three of the greatest rock guitar players of all time: Eric Clapton, Jeff Beck, and Jimmy Page. And they all played Telecasters in the band. So you'd have these pop songs but somewhere in the middle you'd get these incredibly cool guitar solos like nothing you'd ever heard before. And these were played and recorded on Telecasters. Listen to "Shapes of Things" from 1966 and Jeff Beck's guitar at the end with all the distortion, feedback, and crashing sounds. That changed pop music.

Beck later gave his Telecaster to Jimmy Page when he joined the Yardbirds. Page was still playing that same Telecaster when he recorded the first Led Zeppelin album.

Not long ago I went to see Jeff Beck in Vancouver, and he played a Fender Stratocaster all night and was amazing. He hardly spoke throughout the show, he just played his guitar. But for one song and only one song, he picked up his Telecaster, and he just made it cry and weep. The song was by Stevie Wonder entitled "'Cause We've Ended As Lovers" from Jeff's breakthrough guitar instrumental album *Blow by Blow*. I never ever tire of hearing that song.

On much of the Guess Who's *It's Time* album in early 1966 I was using a Fender Telecaster that had this incredible grungy sound through this tiny Fender amp. As a result, much of the material on that album has a biting guitar sound. I didn't have the clean Rickenbacker sound like on our previous albums. Usually you tend to write for your singer, and suddenly I could write for another singer's style, not just Chad Allan's. I could write for Burton Cummings, who had a raw, screamy voice. Now we had an Eric Burdon in the band. So "Believe Me" was like the Kinks and Paul Revere and the Raiders, and "Clock on the Wall" was like the Animals' "House of the Rising Sun" done slower. That was Burton's first vocal with us. Neil Young once told me that "Clock on the Wall" was one of his favourite songs from that period. He even wanted to record it at one time.

Back in the 60s I went to the Winnipeg Arena to see Lonnie Mack. He was a well-known guitar player at the time, so before he comes out on stage, a drummer and a bass player come out and plug in. Then Lonnie comes out and he's got the weirdest-shaped guitar I'd ever seen. It's a Gibson Flying V guitar, sometimes known as a wedge guitar, and it's got a Bigsby tailpiece on it. Along with this guitar around his neck, he's carrying in his hand a Magnatone amplifier. It was small enough for him to carry it like a book. He sets this little amp on a chair, plugs it in, and gets the most amazing sound from it. The amp is vibrating from the volume but it sounds great. I was enthralled by the sound and by his guitar.

So I get the idea that I'm going to have a Flying V guitar like Lonnie Mack. My dad was in the process of finishing our new house; we were moving from West Kildonan to Garden City, just a little farther north. The doors had been delivered for the new house. So I took what was supposed to be my new bedroom door, carried it down to the basement, and cut it in half. On each half I drew a V with a pencil and then cut them out with a saw. We didn't have a router or anything like that, so on one of the V's I cut out where the pickup would be dropped in. I had a Fender Telecaster that didn't work very well and it was all in pieces. So I dropped the Telecaster pickup into the body then added the Fender neck and bridge. I then screwed the two pieces together and I had a Flying V guitar.

My father came home from work that night and I proudly showed him my guitar like a kid showing his dad his woodworking project. "Hey, Dad, isn't it good?" My dad looked at it and then at me and said, "Where did you get that wood?!"

"I found it leaning against my wall."

Then he said, "That was your bedroom door!"

But I played it for many years. It looked like a Gibson Flying V but sounded like a Fender. It's in the National Archives of Canada now.

I have a 1952 Telecaster in my collection. Up to that point they were single-pickup models before they made the Esquire.

The Fender Telecaster is still around today and still reasonably priced. There are lots of imitators, which I guess is a form of flattery, but there's only one Telecaster. It has a sound you cannot help but identify.

## FENDER STRATOCASTER

The Fender Stratocaster debuted in 1954. Leo Fender was looking to create a solid-body guitar with a vibrato arm on it: the early whammy bar. Paul Bigsby had already built a guitar with his patented vibrato, so Leo Fender wanted one as well. With the Bigsby, the strings went over the bridge or saddle and into the tailpiece itself so that you could waver the pitch. Leo Fender put a spring unit in where the strings went through the body, and pulling on the spring-mounted arm allowed you to get a vibrato effect.

The vibrato on Stevie Ray Vaughn's Stratocaster is wound so tight that it only goes down. Instead of wavering the pitch of the note or chord up and down, the spring only lowers the pitch then springs right back in tune. That's a trick Eddie Van Halen uses, too.

The first Stratocasters were all slightly different from each other because they were handmade one at a time. The first time I ever heard a Stratocaster was with Buddy Holly and the Crickets, and the first time I ever saw one was on *American Bandstand* when Jerry Lee Lewis was the guest. His guitar player, Roland James, was playing a Stratocaster.

The Stratocaster sound was just a little thinner than the Telecaster's. It had three single-coil pickups with a selector switch that allowed you to choose which pickup you wanted. But if you weren't careful sometimes you could move the switch just between two positions and get a whole new sound, known as an out-of-phase sound, where you were getting the partial sound of the two pickups blending together. It was a very cool sound that wasn't intentional then, but nowadays it's the sound of guys like John Mayer and Mark Knopfler of Dire Straits. At the time, no other guitar sounded like what an out-of-phase Stratocaster sounded like. Today, though, most Stratocaster models have a five-way switch to give you that sound easily. Hank Marvin played a Fender Stratocaster. He initially wanted to order an American guitar, a Fender Telecaster. But what he got sent to him instead was a fiesta-red Stratocaster. That was the first Fender Stratocaster in the U.K. and the one he used on every Shadows recording.

The thing about the Stratocaster is the wonderful array of sounds you can get from it. Back in the 60s, that sound range was extraordinary. While the Telecaster is more in your face and thicker, the Stratocaster is a little thinner but a lot more varied and versatile in sound.

Jimi Hendrix kind of revived the Stratocaster in the late 60s. Not many guitarists were playing Stats until he came along. He played his upside down because he was left handed. In more recent years, another guitarist who took the Stratocaster to new heights is Mark Knopfler. Not only did he get a unique out-of-phase tone, but he played it with his thumb and fingers, which also gave it a distinctive sound. You can tell it's Mark Knopfler right away as soon as you hear that guitar.

I wrote and recorded "Let It Ride" with BTO on my old Stratocaster. I wrote the song in New Orleans when we were on tour opening for the Doobie Brothers. If you listen to the opening chords you can hear that clean Strat sound.

There's something about the Strat sound that just rings out. If you take that same guitar and run it through a small tweed Fender amp cranked right up, you get a really great bluesy sound. That's what Irish guitarist Rory Gallagher did and got a very distinctive blues sound. We played a lot of shows in a lot of dives with Rory Gallagher in the early 70s, back in the days when BTO was just getting going. Rory would come into the dressing room—we also shared a lot of dressing rooms—in clothes just like us and then change into a funky old flannel shirt and ripped jeans. He was dressing the part of a poor blues guy. Here we are putting all these clothes on to make ourselves look cool onstage and he's dressing down to look funky and streetwise. We got to know Rory quite well. He had a 1950s Stratocaster that was so worn that most of the paint had peeled off, eaten away by thousands of hours of sweat playing in clubs all over the world. But what a sound he got from that old Strat and little amp.

I had a Fender Stratocaster guitar back in the late 60s and I wanted it to sound like many other guitars. So I took a chisel to it and made room for a Telecaster pickup by the bridge and a Gibson Les Paul humbucking pickup farther down the body towards the neck. I left the middle Stratocaster pickup on it. So I could get a Telecaster, Stratocaster, or Gibson Les Paul sound all from the same guitar with just the flick of a switch. That was called my "Legend" guitar. It's lost now, unfortunately. It was stolen.

### GIBSON GUITARS

In the 1940s and 50s guitars began to be miked or amplified. But there were a lot of problems to work out. Acoustic guitars were hollow-bodied and relied on the sound box or body vibrating to get the sound out. But when you placed a pickup on them they often created feedback because the front and back vibrate, and when they do, the pickup vibrates and results in something called a microphonic feedback loop, which is usually an unpleasant squeal. Solid-body guitars eliminated that. But hollow-body electric guitars have a sound that has body to it. It's not just the pickups on a plank of wood. Hollow-body guitars have a rich sound that comes from the bigger body; you can hear the air coming from that body. The thicker the guitar body, the thicker the sound. Gibson was among the first companies to make hollow-body electric guitars. They'd been making acoustic guitars and mandolins since the turn of the century.

Chuck Berry had that thick, fat hollow-body guitar sound. He used a big blond Gibson L5 jazz guitar with black P90 pickups. P90s were single-coil pickups inside a black plastic cover that had a little triangle on top to screw it into the body. They were called "dog's ear pickups" because they looked like the ear of a dog. I just called that Gibson model a Chuck Berry guitar. He played it in all the early rock 'n' roll movies. But if you turned those guitars up too loud they'd still give you feedback because of the hollow body.

Les Paul was trying to stop his big-body jazz guitar from feeding back. So he got a piece of wood he called "The Log," put a pickup on it and a bridge, strings, frets, and tuning pegs, and took it to Gibson and said, "I want you to manufacture this." They said no because to them it looked like a fence post or a plank of wood with a pickup. Les then went to a pawn shop, bought a cheap arch-top guitar, and sliced it right down the middle from the neck to beyond the bridge. He put half on one side of the log and half on the other so that it looked like a guitar. But the real guts of the thing was still the log. Les took it to Gibson, and this time they agreed to make it.

But they soon realized that the body wasn't important to the sound, so they started making just the solid-body guitar, or the Les Paul guitar.

The first Gibson Les Paul guitars looked like a regular Spanish guitar but smaller, as if it had been shrunk down, and made out of solid wood. They were still using the P90 single-coil pickups that could create feedback, so Les decided to take two single-coil pickups, rewire them together, and place them side by side. This cancelled out the hum that would cause the feedback, so they were named humbucking pickups. They bucked or got rid of the hum. The Les Paul Standard solid-body guitar with humbucking pickups became the standard-bearer for rock guitar. It had a much different sound than a Fender or a Gretsch, especially when played through a Marshall amplifier. There's nothing like it. It's the sound of hard rock. One of the best examples of that sound is "All Right Now" by Free with Paul Kossoff playing a 1959 Les Paul Standard through a Marshall stack.

The Gibson Les Paul guitar is the pick 'n' shovel of rock 'n' roll guitars, the ultimate in rock guitars. Whether it's a gold top or a sunburst ('burst), they sound the same. Jimmy Page played a 1959 Les Paul in Led Zeppelin that was given to him by Joe Walsh.

He was able to get sounds out of his Les Paul that nobody else gets because the pickups were put in backwards and so produce this cool out-of-phase sound. He was able to reverse the polarity in his pickups and get a very distinctive sound, the sound of Led Zeppelin.

Peter Green, of early Fleetwood Mac and before that John Mayall's Bluesbreakers, gave his 1955 Les Paul to Irish blues rock guitarist Gary Moore in the mid 70s. That guitar recently sold for $1 million. The previous owner who sold it to Peter Green was the Rolling Stones' Keith Richards.

I have a 1959 Gibson Les Paul with a Bigsby vibrato tailpiece. I still play that guitar to this day and it's probably worth $250,000 to $300,000. That's the guitar I played the lead on for "American Woman." It's amazing that a guitar that probably cost $350 new is now worth hundreds of thousands of dollars. Once you play certain hits with these guitars, they take on a life of their own.

In the late 60s the Guess Who played a lot around Vancouver and the West Coast, and that's where I acquired my Gibson Les Paul. I'd broken my Rickenbacker and was using a blue sparkle Mosrite, which was a funny-shaped guitar that the Ventures used. It looked cool, but the neck was like a bow and arrow. I had it along when we played a church basement gig in Nanaimo. We were onstage playing our set when from the back of the hall came a young man with a little brown guitar case. I knew what was in that case; every guitar player back then knew what a Les Paul case looked like. The Les Paul guitar was the sound of Eric Clapton on the *John Mayall's Bluesbreakers* album, and of Cream, Jimmy Page in Led Zeppelin, and Peter Green—the heavy blues-rock sound.

The kid opened the case and I could see it was an original '59 Les Paul with a factory-installed Bigsby tailpiece. He gestured at the Mosrite and back to the Les Paul. I knew what he wanted. In mid-song I took off the Mosrite, he handed me the Les Paul, and I tuned it up and played it the rest of the night. It had incredible sound. It was heavy to hold, but it rocked. After the show I handed it back to him, saying thanks for letting me play his guitar.

"You mean you don't want to trade with me?" he asked, surprised.

"What?! You want to trade me your Les Paul for my Mosrite?" He then told me how he'd seen me playing the Mosrite on television and wanted a guitar like that. His uncle had given him the Les Paul and the kid didn't think it was very cool.

"Just a minute. This isn't a fair trade," I told him. "I've got $75 in my pocket. I'll trade you the Mosrite and $75, but I want someone to witness the deal and to sign a paper attesting that we both agreed to the trade."

The minister witnessed the exchange and signed the paper. The kid went home happy and I got the guitar that would become the sound of "No Time" and "American Woman." That guitar became associated with my sound, the sound of the Guess Who.

Many years later while I was playing in BTO, out of the blue I received a letter from a lawyer seeking redress, claiming I had taken advantage of the kid who was now his client. I sent him a copy of the paper signed by the minister and never heard back from him.

Neil Young has this old black Gibson Les Paul that he's had absolutely forever, at least since the late 60s, but it's a 1950s model Les Paul. It has a Bigsby vibrato tailpiece on it because Neil likes to use vibrato. He's kept the original neck pickup since it has a fatter tone, very bassy, which Les Pauls have. But he replaced the bridge pickup with a Gibson Firebird guitar pickup, which is wound differently and sounds different from a standard humbucking pickup. It has a more trebly sound, brighter. He calls this guitar Old Black; it's his main guitar and has been for decades. If you listen to "Down by the River" you can hear him switching from one pickup to the other and the differences in sound.

As experiments, Gibson made a bunch of weirdly shaped guitars in the late 50s and early 60s, including the Flying V, the Firebird, and the Explorer. But they made only a few of these models because they didn't sell. Today they're worth a fortune. A kid's father bought him an Explorer back in 1960. The kid didn't want it, so he put it in its case and left it under his bed. Decades later he found the guitar in the ruins of his parents' house following a hurricane. The house was destroyed, but the guitar was in perfect shape and had never been played. He contacted an auction house, which sold this original Gibson Explorer with a factory-installed Bigsby for $610,000.

### GRETSCH GUITARS

The first Gretsch guitar I ever saw and heard played was by Lenny Breau, or Lone Pine Jr., as he was called by his dad in their band. He had a big orange Gretsch with a big black letter G burned into the body like a brand on a cow. It was called a Gretsch 6120 Chet Atkins G brand model. When I talked to Lenny he told me who the guitar was named after: Mr. Chet Atkins. I saved money for years to buy one just like that. I babysat, mowed lawns, and delivered papers to save up $400, a lot of money in 1961, for an orange Gretsch 6120 Chet Atkins like Lenny's. Neil Young and other guys did the same thing, saving to buy a Gretsch Chet Atkins. I bought mine from Eddie Laham at Winnipeg Piano Co. on Portage Avenue. I played that guitar on "Shakin' All Over" and on "Takin' Care of Business." It had that depth in it and wasn't as shallow-sounding as a solid-body guitar. The Gretsch guitar has a beautiful mid-range twang that's different from Fenders or Gibsons.

Gretsch came out with a pickup that also cancelled out the hum from single-coil pickups. But since Gibson had already patented or trademarked the name humbucker or humbucking, Gretsch couldn't use it. So instead they named their humbucking pickups "Filtertron" pickups. They did the same thing, filtered out the hum.

I had one of the only orange Gretsch 6120 models in Winnipeg. The other one was owned by Johnny Glowa, who used to be the lead guitar player in the Silvertones before me. He couldn't make the payments, though, so Neil Young's mom, Rassy, bought it for Neil in 1963. Neil still plays an orange 6120, but not that one, which he traded in for a Gibson twelve-string acoustic guitar in Toronto in 1965. He's regretted that ever since. But when the Buffalo Springfield was formed the next year, the first thing he bought was another orange Gretsch 6120 that he still plays today.

The sound of the Buffalo Springfield and Crosby, Stills, Nash and Young was the sound of Neil Young and Stephen Stills playing Gretsch 6120s or White Falcons, duelling back and forth. The White Falcon was the top-of-the-line Gretsch model introduced in the late 50s.

On the original Johnny Kidd recording of "Shakin' All Over" the guitar player used a cigarette lighter to get that wavering sound when the band stops just before the chorus. But I was able to use my Bigsby vibrato on my Gretsch 6120 to make the chord waver.

Chet Atkins learned to play guitar by ear, no formal lessons. When he started recording albums of guitar instrumentals featuring him on the cover playing a Gretsch guitar, it inspired so many young guitarists to buy a Gretsch. They were like the Cadillac of guitars, the high-end models, and were priced higher than Fenders or Gibsons. Chet Atkins did country picking on his Gretsch, but when you took that same guitar and put it in the hands of an early rock 'n' roller like Eddie Cochran, you got a whole different sound. Eddie's first guitar was a Gibson that had a P90 "dog's ear pickup" on it. These were bassier sounding pickups. But when he got his Gretsch, he liked the twangy sound but still wanted that bassy tone, too, because often guys didn't have bass players and had to play the bass parts on guitar. So Eddie Cochran took a P90 pickup from a Gibson and put it on his orange Gretsch Chet Atkins 6120 as the forward pickup to get that bassy "Summertime Blues" and "Come On Everybody" sound. You can see it in early photos of him. That was his sound. He still had the twangy Gretsch pickup for lead, though.

Chet Atkins actually didn't like his 6120 guitar. It was made for him rather than designed by him, and he needed a wider neck for his finger-picking style. He was known in the music business as the Country Gentleman, so when he did design a guitar that fit all his needs, it was called the Country Gentleman. At first it was a single cutaway with the F holes filled in with plastic so that it wouldn't create feedback as hollow-body guitars tended to do. It also had a bigger body than the 6120, and was done in a beautiful dark mahogany finish. To get more clearance on it the later models had two cutaways, a double cutaway model. The double cutaway Gretsch Country Gentleman was introduced in the early 60s, but wasn't a big seller. Then the Beatles appeared on *The Ed Sullivan Show* in 1964 with George Harrison playing a double cutaway Country Gentleman. "All My Loving" has a Chet Atkins–style solo in it. All of a sudden Gretsch Country Gentleman sales went through the roof. Fred Gretsch owes a lot to George Harrison for popularizing his guitars.

Mr. Twang himself, Duane Eddy, created his own unique sound to be different from everybody else. He had a Gretsch Chet Atkins guitar like many others in early rock. He didn't want any distortion in his sound. If you turn your guitar up full and turn your amplifier up as well, you get buzzy-sounding distortion. Nowadays guitar players want that sound, but back in the 50s they didn't. Duane Eddy had heard the clean sound of a Fender guitar and he wanted that, too. He also had an Echoplex to give his guitar an echo sound, and he restricted his playing to the lower frets and a bassier sound using heavier strings. He worked with his producer, Lee Hazlewood, to refine this distinctive sound. They used a bass guitar amplifier with a giant fifteen-inch speaker so that when they turned it up it wouldn't distort. Smaller speakers tended to distort more easily. Then they took the back off the amplifier and filled in the cabinet with fibreglass so that the speaker wouldn't resonate. They also added a slight tremolo, which is where the sound appears to be going off and on quickly, as well as some reverb to give it depth. And from all that they got the sound of Duane Eddy and his twangy guitar. Listen to "Rebel Rouser" and you'll hear that very sound. It's as if he's playing in a cave a mile away. He used to say, "The twang's the thang!" Duane Eddy also did a lot to promote Gretsch guitars and had his own model named for him.

Gene Vincent's lead guitar player, Cliff Gallup, originally played a Gretsch guitar. But he didn't play a big hollow-body Chet Atkins model. Instead, he played what was a copy of a Gibson Les Paul solid-body guitar called a Duo Jet or Rock Jet. George Harrison played one in the very early Beatles, and he's pictured with one on the cover of his solo album *Cloud Nine*. Cliff Gallup played his Duo Jet on Gene Vincent's "Be-Bop-A-Lula."

Bo Diddley played a Gretsch Rock Jet but, just to be different, he had Gretsch make him a rectangle-shaped model. It was a deep red, and with all the gear on it, it looked like a Christmas present. Bo Diddley would tune his guitar to an E chord so that all he had to do was bar it anywhere up the neck. That's how he got his sound. Gretsch has since reissued Bo Diddley's rectangle guitar.

### RICKENBACKER GUITARS

Listen to the beginning of "A Hard Day's Night." That's the chord that shook the world. Imagine playing one chord and every-body around the world instantly knowing what's coming after it and knowing what song it is. It's the most amazing chord that George Harrison plays—a suspended chord on a twelve-string Rickenbacker guitar that has a lot more high strings on it. Most twelve-string guitars had the low string first in the double strings, but Rickenbackers reversed that. Having the high string first gave it a more jingle-jangly sound, which became a signature sound of the Rickenbacker twelve-string electric guitar.

When the Beatles were in New York to play *The Ed Sullivan Show* in February 1964 George Harrison was presented with a Rickenbacker 360 Deluxe. That was only the second one made, and that's the one he played on "A Hard Day's Night." He also played it on "You Can't Do That," which was filmed for the movie but didn't make the cut.

The sole identifiable sound of the Byrds was Jim (Roger) McGuinn's Rickenbacker 360 twelve-string guitar. He played it through a compressor and cranked up the treble. When you do that you get the sound of mid-60s folk rock, that jingle-jangle "Mr. Tambourine Man" folk rock sound. The Byrds invented the sound that everyone copied after that. McGuinn saw George Harrison playing a Rickenbacker twelve-string in the movie *A Hard Day's Night* and went out and got one when the Byrds were just starting out. He used finger picks because he'd been a folkie before the Byrds. They took a Bob Dylan song, "Mr. Tambourine Man," and changed the world with it.

I had a Rickenbacker guitar, a 360 six-string model. It looked like McGuinn's, only it had six strings and was black. Chad Allan played the little John Lennon Rickenbacker model, a three-quarter-size guitar. Rickenbackers had so much clarity. The pickups were originally designed for lap steel guitars, for Hawaiian music, so they had a very clear, clean, high trebly sound. Listen to Creedence Clearwater Revival and John Fogerty playing one of those smaller John Lennon Rickenbackers; he gets a very clear trebly sound. That became his signature sound and style. You can really hear that sound on Creedence's "Up Around the Bend" or "Fortunate Son." Not as twangy and sharp as a Fender Telecaster, but very clear and clean. That's the sound of swamp rock.

### RANDY'S GUITAR COLLECTION

When my Gretsch 6120 was stolen from my car while I was in Toronto mixing BTO's last album, *Freeways*, I offered a reward for it but never found it. What resulted instead was that I started collecting Gretsch guitars. It became a routine for me in every city or town I was in on the road to scour the pawnshops and vintage guitar collectors in search of my Gretsch. In doing this I started buying different Gretsch models. What began as a search for my lost guitar became a hobby to pass the time on the road. That then turned into an obsession. I wanted to own as many Gretsch guitars as possible. It was my midlife-crisis diversion, collecting guitars. And I approached it with a fixation. It became the thrill of the hunt for me and gave me a great deal of pleasure.

Wherever I went I checked out guitars. I had contacts notifying me if a particular Gretsch model came across their counter or if they heard about someone with a rare model. At first I asked to be notified only if they found my original orange Gretsch, but they started calling if any Gretsch came their way. My curiosity would be piqued, I'd go see what they had, and more often than not I'd buy it. I became known as "the Gretsch Guy" or "Gretsch Guru"—collectors and dealers would call me whenever they found one. I wasn't a "Gretsch-aholic" with a family waiting for me to come home with money for food and instead I'd spent it on a guitar. I just spent extra money I had. My wife, Denise, got into it as well. She'd be in San Francisco visiting family and would make a detour to a second-hand guitar shop. She'd call me if they had any interesting Gretsch model.

I still have players or dealers show up backstage at my gigs with rare guitars for me. I don't just buy Gretsches; I collect Gibsons and Fenders, too. On the Van Halen tour, Eddie and I would be playfully fighting over these guitars that dealers brought in.

When I lived in White Rock, B.C., I had my entire Gretsch collection on the walls of my big basement room, and it was stunning to walk into that room. I remember taking Fred Gretsch there just to see the look on his face. It was unbelievable. I had a white wall of all white Gretsch Penguins and Falcons, an orange wall of Duane Eddy 6120s, a coloured wall of Sparkle Jet models, a blond wall. It was insanely over the top, but I loved it.

When I moved, I didn't want just any moving guys to pack them up. I rented a truck and I hired my son Brigham and my nephew Paxton, my brother Timmy's son, to pack each guitar individually in its case. We had hundreds of cases spread out on the driveway and the boys matched guitar to case. They'd look at a closed case and say "What's in that one?" and open it to find some exotic, one-of-a-kind guitar, a Black Falcon or a Penguin. My collection was recently sold to the Gretsch company for exhibit purposes. I never did find my lost 6120, though. Soon you'll be able to see the "Bachman Gretsch Collection" at the Georgia Music Hall of Fame and Museum.

### BURNS GUITARS

Although not necessarily a staple guitar like a Stratocaster or a Gretsch, Burns guitars have a special history. The Shadows had the perfect blend of lead and rhythm guitars, bass and drums. A few years after the Shadows were going strong they made a deal with Burns guitars in the U.K. to play their guitars. Burns designed a special Hank Marvin model with big horns on it, a vibrato arm, and a kind of scrolled headstock. On the headstock it was inscribed with Hank Marvin's name. I'm lucky enough to have a white 1964 Burns Hank Marvin guitar. Right after that Burns went out of business. So they only made a few of those. Jim Burns passed away and the company went bankrupt. They closed the warehouse and the company sat in litigation for some forty years. But when Jim Burns's son came of age, he untangled the legal mess and was able to get the Burns Guitars trademark back. He resurrected the factory and started making guitars under the Burns name again.

I had a friend in the U.K. named Trevor Wilkinson who was a Shadows fan and also a good friend of the Burns family. Trevor took me to the old Burns warehouse that had been padlocked for decades and opened it up, and there were four guitars on the bench. "Do you want one?" he asked me. "Absolutely!" They weren't finished yet, so he asked me what colour I wanted. I told him I wanted a white one just like Hank's. Trevor got a red one and I got a white one. I took the pick guard from that Burns guitar with me when I went to see the Shadows and got Hank and Bruce Welch to sign it.

## My Picks

"ALL MY LOVING" by the Beatles

"ALL RIGHT NOW" by Free

"AMERICAN WOMAN" by the Guess Who

"BE-BOP-A-LULA" by Gene Vincent and the Blue Caps

"BELIEVE ME" by the Guess Who

"CARAVAN" by Les Paul and Mary Ford

"CAUSE WE'VE ENDED AS LOVERS" by Jeff Beck

"CLOCK ON THE WALL" by the Guess Who

"DON'T MAKE MY BABY BLUE" by the Shadows

"DOWN BY THE RIVER" by Neil Young and Crazy Horse

"FOR WHAT IT'S WORTH" by the Buffalo Springfield

"A HARD DAY'S NIGHT" by the Beatles

"HEY BO DIDDLEY" by Bo Diddley

"I FEEL FREE" by Cream

"I WALK THE LINE" by Johnny Cash and the Tennessee Two

"JOHNNY B. GOODE" by Chuck Berry

"LET IT RIDE" by BTO

"LONG TRAIN RUNNIN'" by the Doobie Brothers

"LOTTA LOVIN'" by Gene Vincent and the Blue Caps

"MR. TAMBOURINE MAN" by the Byrds

"OH BY JINGO" by Chet Atkins

"REBEL ROUSER" by Duane Eddy

"SHAKIN' ALL OVER" by the Guess Who

"SHAKIN' ALL OVER" by Johnny Kidd and the Pirates

"SULTANS OF SWING" by Dire Straits

"SUMMERTIME BLUES" by Eddie Cochran

"SUSIE Q" by Dale Hawkins

"TURN! TURN! TURN!" by the Byrds

"UP AROUND THE BEND" by Creedence Clearwater Revival

"THE WIND CRIES MARY" by the Jimi Hendrix Experience

"WONDERFUL LAND" by the Shadows

"YOU CAN'T DO THAT" by the Beatles

# Close Encounters of the Six-String Kind, Part 1

I'm a bit of a rock 'n' roll gadfly. I've been fortunate to be seren-dipitously at the right place at the right time to meet many of the movers and shakers in rock music. I've met many of my heroes or artists I respect as influences, and I'm often surprised that they know who I am. I've reminisced about many of those encounters over the years on *Vinyl Tap*. Here are some of the highlights.

## GENE VINCENT

After Elvis Presley's success in the mid 50s, record labels went in search of Elvis clones, young rock 'n' roll singers with an edgy attraction. America's Gene Vincent was one of those early rockers who was discovered and launched as a post-Elvis teenage phenom-enon. But he wasn't just a copyist; Gene Vincent had the goods. "Be-Bop-A-Lula" is his signature song, a true rock 'n' roll classic.

I remember reading in one of the Winnipeg newspapers that Gene Vincent and the Blue Caps were playing the Dominion Theatre downtown near Portage and Main. They'd be playing three consecutive days in a row in April. This would have been 1958. Needless to say, I wanted to be there for every show. It was the closest I was ever going to get to Elvis. Gene Vincent had a guitar player in the Blue Caps named Cliff Gallup who became very influential. Jeff Beck even recorded a tribute album to Cliff Gallup. I would buy Gene Vincent records because they were so similar to Elvis—very simple chord structures but really wild stuff.

At the time back in Winnipeg I had a friend named Victor Zahn who owned an old army-brown Harley Davidson motorcycle he'd bought from army surplus. Victor used to ride around town on the Harley with me on the back. My parents would never let me own a motorcycle! When Gene Vincent came to town, Victor Zahn and I hopped on his Harley and drove down to the Dominion Theatre. At that time Gene Vincent had three songs on the Winnipeg record charts on both radio stations: "Be-Bop-A-Lula," "Dance to the Bop," and "Lotta Lovin'." The Dominion Theatre must have held about eighteen hundred people, but that night there were maybe thirty-five people in the audience, including Victor and me. Gene and the Blue Caps came out and did the most incredible set.

It really was no big deal back then to go backstage and get autographs, so Victor and I went to meet Gene Vincent and his band. We were the only ones. I told Gene that it was too bad he was booked to play Winnipeg this particular weekend. He said, "What do you mean?" When you're on the road you tend to lose track of days. It was Good Friday and Sunday was Easter. Passover was around then, too. Back then Winnipeg was a fairly strict city with plenty of religious groups and denominations, so on Good Friday everything was shut down except for the theatres, I guess for all the non-Christians. Gene made a couple of phone calls and cancelled his Sunday gig, but he kept the Saturday gig, which I went to as well.

After Friday's show we were all standing around talking in the back alley of the theatre, and Victor went to get his motorcycle. As soon as he saw it Gene Vincent said, "I wanna ride it!" All the guys in his band are yelling, "No! No!" Gene had a brace on his leg from breaking his shin bone in a motorcycle accident. But now that it was healed he wanted to get back on the horse. He wanted to get on the Harley. So Victor let him ride on the back for about twenty feet and then asked, "Is that enough?" Gene said, "No. I've gotta have a long ride on this motorcycle." At that point we had to go home, but said we'd see them the next night.

We came back the next night and the band let us back in because we didn't have enough money for another night's tickets. We sat through the show and again there were very few people in the audience. Like the night before, they came out and played an incredible show as if the place was packed. Afterwards I asked Gene what he was doing now that he'd cancelled the Sunday show for Easter, and he said they were just going to hang around in the hotel.

"Would you like to come over to my house for Easter dinner?" I asked him.

And he replied, "Will your friend give me a ride on his Harley?" Again, the band is saying, "No, don't do it! You can't get on another motorcycle!"

So I went home and told my mom that we were having another seat at the table for Easter dinner, a musician friend of mine. That was no big deal to her because with four boys in the family, we were always bringing friends home for dinner. The next afternoon Victor pulls up in his Harley and, sure enough, there's Gene Vincent on the back. Unfortunately he couldn't stay for dinner because the guys in his band were freaking out about him on a motorcycle and he had to get back. But he gave me his blue cap and signed it, and I still have it. He signed it in ballpoint pen and the signature has faded. But that was my brush with Gene Vincent. He was a great singer, a nice guy, and pretty normal.

## JOHNNY AND THE HURRICANES

Behind the Hudson's Bay Company store downtown was the Winnipeg Auditorium, which used to be a great place for concerts.

I remember seeing the Supremes there, wrestling matches, Ferlin Husky, Johnny Cash. We once opened for Eric Burdon and the Animals there, and Burton Cummings played an electric harpsichord that night on "His Girl" and "A Wednesday in Your Garden." And I remember I saw Johnny and the Hurricanes from Ohio at the Auditorium.

They had a hit out called "Crossfire," and in the Red River Valley they had a hit with "Red River Rock" with sax and organ playing the melody lines. Instrumental music was the big thing then; everybody loved it. Back in those days I'd take a notebook and a pen with me and would always try to get a seat in the front row so that I could watch the guitar players. I'd take notes on what they were doing, where they put their fingers on the neck, and how they did it, like "fifth fret slide to eighth fret on top two strings." Then I'd go home and try playing it from my notes. Nowadays, kids buy or download videos of how to play guitar and specific solos, but there was nothing like that back then.

So when Johnny and the Hurricanes came to town I was there in the front row with my notebook. I wanted to watch how the guitar player, Dave Yorko, did the slide line in the middle of "Crossfire." He had a beautiful red Gibson double cutaway with a Bigsby vibrato tailpiece. But every time it came to a guitar-lead part he'd turn his back to the audience. I couldn't see what he was playing. After the show I went backstage, hoping he would show me how he did his solos. But Dave Yorko wasn't a very nice guy. I thought that maybe if I was nice to him backstage he'd show me how he did his solos.

Then I heard Johnny, who went by the name Johnny Paris but was really Johnny Pucisk, tell someone that he couldn't get any decent Polish food in Winnipeg. It turned out that the guys in the band all had a Polish or Ukrainian background. So I said, "Hey, my mother's Ukrainian. Do you want her to make you some perogies and stuff?" and Johnny and the guys went, "Yeah!" So I went home that night and got my mother, who was a Dobrinsky of Polish-Ukrainian background from the North End, to make up some perogies and holopchi, and I took them to Johnny and the Hurricanes, who were thrilled. As I'm giving out these cabbage rolls and sausages to Johnny, Dave Yorko is there, looking on hungrily. He was a Ukrainian guy, too. So I said to him, "Why do you turn your back when you take a solo?" and he replied, "Because I don't want anyone to see the solos I make up." So I said, "If you just show me where you put your fingers on the fretboard, you can have some of this food." So it became a tradeoff: He got some food, and I got to see how to play the guitar leads on the Johnny and the Hurricanes songs.

It was perogies that also led me to meet legendary movie actor/comedian Danny Kaye in the early 70s. BTO had recorded their first album at RCA studios in Toronto. We were still Brave Belt then, but *Brave Belt III* instead became *BTO I*. So when it came time to record the second BTO album, I checked out a studio opening in Seattle, just south of Vancouver. It was called Kaye-Smith Studios, but not after the 40s and 50s singer Kay Smith. The Smith was Lester Smith, a broadcaster who owned many radio stations, and the Kaye was actor and comedian Danny Kaye.

I went to the opening of the studio, and because Danny Kaye was Ukrainian Jewish they had knishes and perogies. Now, I could relate to that because my family was pretty much all Ukrainian, and in the North End of Winnipeg and West Kildonan where I grew up just about everyone was Ukrainian or Jewish. Most of my friends as a kid were Jewish. So what could be a better studio opening?! I met Danny Kaye that day and he was a really nice guy. It was a thrill for me, having seen his movies as a kid, although he had no idea who I was. He was very funny in person. I was impressed with his studio, and we ended up recording two BTO albums at Kaye-Smith Studios in Seattle.

## BOBBY CURTOLA

It's fair to say that Bobby Curtola was Canada's first rock 'n' roll teen idol. He began his career selling his records from the trunk of his car and touring the country using local bands to back him up. Bobby was from Thunder Bay—back then it was called Port Arthur. He was a big Canadian pop star at the time, with several hit records such as "Fortune Teller" and "Three Rows Over." They used to play his records on the radio in Winnipeg and I remember thinking, "Man, if someone so close to us can make it"—Port Arthur was about an eight-hour drive east—"then maybe I could, too!"

He even had his own record label at the time, Tartan Records. So when Bobby asked us, Chad Allan and the Reflections, to be his backing band, it was a big thrill and a big deal at the time. He was a great singer and wrote his own songs. He was a smart cookie. We played the Calgary Stampede and Klondike Days with Bobby. He even had a sponsorship deal with Coca-Cola, so we played the Coca-Cola Teen Tent with him. Bobby recorded the first Coca-Cola rock 'n' roll jingle, something the Guess Who did a few years later. But Bobby was the first. When we backed him up, the girls used to scream like crazy for him. Amazingly enough, recently we were in the Bay out here on the West Coast buying a watch for my daughter Callianne's birthday, and the woman who sold it to us said that she remembered seeing me playing with Bobby Curtola at the Teen Tent back in 1963. How's that for a memory!

## LES PAUL

I remember in the late 50s hearing that the great Les Paul was coming to Winnipeg to play the Rancho Don Carlos out on Pembina Highway in the south end of Winnipeg. I'd heard all those wonderful Les Paul and Mary Ford records like "Vaya con Dios" and "How High the Moon" with all the multi-tracked guitars, and I loved what he did, although I didn't know how he did it at the time. And every guitar player was well aware of Gibson's line of Les Paul solid-body guitars. I knew I had to see him live just to see how he was able to get those amazing guitar sounds. It was a two-hour bus ride from West Kildonan, and when I finally arrived at the club they wouldn't let me in. I was under age; the drinking age then was twenty-one and I was still a teenager. So I was sitting outside the Rancho on the lawn, despondent, when a big Cadillac pulled up. Out comes Les Paul, Mary Ford, and their son (who played drums). Les came up to me and said, "Hi, kid … What's the matter?" I told him I'd come across town on a couple of buses to see him but I was under age and couldn't get in. He talked with the manager, and I was then allowed to stand in the kitchen and watch the show through the big round windows in the swinging kitchen doors, with waiters coming back and forth with trays of food and drinks. But I got to see the show.

Right beside me in the kitchen, stacked on top of each other, were six single-track Ampex tape recorders with a giant cable going out to Les's Gibson Les Paul guitar. On his guitar below the Bigsby tremolo arm were a bunch of switches that he used to stop and start the tape recorders. I stepped out of the kitchen to watch Les as he demonstrated to the audience how he got his sound, this big multi-guitar sound. Nobody in the audience knew what multi-tracking was. They just thought it was some kind of magic. Les explained to them how he used his "Paulverizer" to work the tape recorders and play back what he had played. He'd then play live over that. I was amazed.

After the show, as he was coming back out for another bow, he said to me as he passed by in the kitchen, "Here kid, hold this," and I held his Les Paul guitar. Man, was it heavy. When he came back I asked him if he could show me the lick he played in "How High the Moon." It was a very simple run down the high E string. So he showed me how he played it.

Leap ahead a lifetime and I'm with BTO. It's the 1980s

and we're opening for Van Halen on the 5150 tour. We're at Meadowlands Coliseum. Les Paul came to see the show and came backstage to meet everyone. So I went up to him and said, "Mr. Paul, I met you when I was a teenager in Winnipeg." He looked at me and then said, "Oh yeah! The Rancho Don Carlos, right?" I couldn't believe he remembered. Then he looked at me, smiled, and said, "Here kid, hold this," just like he'd said way back when. I was blown away that he recalled that moment in Winnipeg and the kid in the kitchen, me. He went on to tell me that while everyone else was drinking, eating, or just listening to the music, I was intently watching everything he did, so he figured I was a guitar player. Then he said, "Do you still know the lick?" I did and played it for him in the dressing room.

Fast-forward again to September 2001. This time I was in New York to play with the reunited Guess Who with Joe Cocker as the opening act. I was invited to the Iridium Club where Les Paul played every Monday night. It was amazing to see him again. Halfway through his set he says, "There's a dear friend of mine out in the audience who I've known since he was a kid." I'm wondering who he's talking about. Then he says, "This kid grew up to be a bit famous, and I'm going to invite him up to play a few songs. Would Randy Bachman please join me onstage." I was stunned. The crowd applauded as I made my way up to the front where I was handed a black Les Paul guitar. Together with Les and his drummer, we played "How High the Moon" and I did the lick he'd shown me way back in Winnipeg so many years ago. Then he said, "Okay, kid, let's play one of your songs." So I played a bluesy shuffle version of "Takin' Care of Business" with Les Paul playing licks that brought the house down.

After the show he invited me out to his place in Mawpah, New Jersey, the next day. I was all set to go the next morning when all hell broke loose. It was 9/11 and the Twin Towers were destroyed and New York City was closed down. So I never got the chance to visit Les Paul at his home and see all his gadgets and gizmos. I regret that tremendously, but cherish the memories I have of this great guitar player, inventor, creator, and all-round nice guy.

### DION AND THE BELMONTS

Dion and the Belmonts were the most successful of the white doo-wop groups out of New York, with hits like "The Wanderer" and "Runaround Sue." They were also the most suave-looking guys. They had cool hair and wore nice suits, and Dion diMucci was a very handsome guy with an incredible vocal delivery. In the summer of 1965 the Guess Who were working out of New York and we were invited to play on the Kingsmen's "Louie Louie" tour. On the tour with us were Dion and the Belmonts. It was a re-formed Belmonts, with some of the original members. I remember a Carlo and a Danny and, of course, Dion.

I thought Dion was the coolest guy. He had a Martin acoustic guitar and they would sit at the back of the tour bus and sing doo-wop songs, snapping their fingers and singing stuff like "Why Must I Be a Teenager in Love." I hung around Dion all the time and watched him. He had such a smooth voice.

Now, when I say tour bus I don't mean the luxury land cruisers that stars have today. Those are like suites at the Hilton Hotel on wheels. Back then it was literally a regular Greyhound bus with bench seats and you tried to sleep on those. Not very comfortable.

I actually got a guitar part that I later used in "Undun" from a Dion song called "Soft Guitar" written by singer/songwriter Kenny Rankin and sung by Dion. It's a cool little turn around two-chord pattern that I used at the end of the verses in "Undun."

### THE CRYSTALS

In the fall of 1965 we were still working out of New York for Scepter Records and would travel from Winnipeg to New York to record or play gigs. We'd back the Shirelles, the Ronettes, and the Crystals at gigs and then play our own set. We were there in New York around American Thanksgiving, which, as all Canadians know, is a month later than our Thanksgiving. Someone said to us, "Where are you going for Thanksgiving dinner?" For us, Thanksgiving was already over. So Dee Dee Kinniebrew from the Crystals invited us over to her house to have Thanksgiving dinner with her family. We didn't know where the girls from the Crystals lived. We were just five white guys from Winnipeg. So they took us to where they lived, a largely black area of New York. I think a lot of the black kids hadn't seen many white people, certainly not Canadian white guys. When we got out of the car the kids in the neighbourhood came over and stared at us. But we went into the house and her parents were very nice to us, and we had a lovely Thanksgiving dinner.

I remember when the Crystals' big record was first released and I was at CKRC radio with Doc Steen. He'd gotten the record but hadn't heard it yet. So he announced it as "Here's the Crystals with Duh Do Run Run" instead of "Da Do Ron Ron."

### THE WHO

I met the Who in 1967 in London. I'd gone there with the Guess Who, but as I talked about earlier, we ended up not doing any gigs there. We heard that the Who were playing the Marquee club in Soho and decided we'd tell them to stop using their name because we were the Guess Who and who did they think they were? The Marquee is a famous London club where Cream and the Stones have played, but it's about the size of a living room. They jammed a hundred and fifty people into it every night shoulder to shoulder. We came in and sat at a table. It was during the day and the Who were filming a television spot, so there was no one else in the club. They had gigantic amplifiers the size of giant refrigerators, these hundred-watt Marshall amps six feet tall with hundreds and hundreds of watts of power blasting out. We could hear them clearly outside on the street before we went in. They were so loud that they had to keep playing the songs over and over again because the excessive volume kept making the film in the cameras flutter. The director kept telling them to turn down. So, of course, the band would turn up just to be defiant. Our ears were ringing as if someone had fired a gun next to our heads. We didn't want to look rude or uncool by plugging our ears, but it was painful. So we were sitting there being blasted over and over by these songs, and by the time they're done we were all deaf.

Once they were finished filming they came over and we talked, and we told them they couldn't continue using their name.

"We need to straighten out the name," I told them. "We're the Guess Who and we're getting confused with you guys."

John Entwistle, their bass player who was known as the Ox, looked us up and down and simply mumbled, "Oh, bugger off. There's the Byrds and Yardbirds so there can be a Who and Guess Who, so bugger off."

That became a running prank between John Entwistle and me. Years later we were staying at the same hotel as the Who, and Jim Kale and I went up to Entwistle's room and knocked on his door at three in the morning. He was in deep sleep and we woke him up.

"Who is it?" he shouted from behind the door.

"It's the Guess Who. Bugger off!" And we ran off laughing. Later we'd phone his room and do it again.

The Guess Who were checking into the Continental Hyatt Hotel in Los Angeles sometime in 1969, and as we were signing the register, the manager asked us the name of our band. We told him "the Guess Who." Moments later two security guards confronted us.

"Unless you pay this outstanding bill for damages, you are not allowed into this hotel and we will prosecute you."

"No, you've got the wrong band," we told him. "We're the *Guess Who*."

If we had been the Who, the hotel would have required us to post a $10,000 bond in case of damages. The group had been banned from just about every American hotel.

"It's not us. We're Canadians." We showed them our passports. So they let us stay.

In the 1990s when John and I met for the Ringo Starr All-Starrs tour, I went up to greet him and said, "I'm Randy Bachman from the Guess Who. Bugger off." He roared with laughter.

After rehearsals with the All-Starr Band in Vancouver, John and I went to the opening of the new Hard Rock Café in Gastown and got to play "Shakin' All Over" together. John was a mild-mannered, soft-spoken guy and we got along great on the tour. I loved playing "Boris the Spider" every night with John.

### JEFFERSON AIRPLANE

I've known the guys in the Jefferson Airplane a long time. We were both signed to RCA Records. The band was formed in San Francisco by Marty Balin, who was a folk singer, but he wanted to rock out more after the Byrds had created folk rock. So he found some other folk players, including Paul Kantner and Jorma Kaukonen, and formed Jefferson Airplane. The Airplane were kind of the ultimate drug band and epitomized that San Francisco hippie drug scene. They were the troubadours of the drug culture.

In November 1967 the Guess Who were booked to open two shows for the Jefferson Airplane. Burton Cummings and I and the rest of the band wanted to be our utmost psychedelic selves. We'd been in England earlier that year, so we thought we would do all our freakiest stuff. I had my Herzog pre-amp unit and my whammy bar and I'd make all these weird feedback sounds. We did Hendrix and Cream songs.

My father was an alderman in West Kildonan and a member of the West Kildonan Legion. The Legion had just acquired a new flag, so he brought the old Union Jack flag home. This was a huge flag. I asked if I could have it, and my dad figured I was just going to hang it on my wall. When we did the first show with the Airplane in Minneapolis they were all wearing these cool kaftans and Nehru clothes, necklaces and beads. We wanted to dress cool, too. So I took the flag, cut a hole in it, and wore it as a poncho on stage at the Winnipeg Arena. I thought I was being pretty cool. I didn't even realize that the next day was Remembrance Day. We played our opening set and I did my psychedelic-sounds stuff while Burton pretended to bow down at my feet. The next day there was all this fuss in the papers and on the radio about this alderman's son who had desecrated the Union Jack by wearing it on stage. I had managed to earn the indignation of war veterans and monarchists throughout the city. My father was furious with me. "What were you thinking?!"

We went out there and pulled out every trick we had. No one in Winnipeg had heard Hendrix or Cream, and we did our own psychedelic songs like "When Friends Fall Out" and "Friends of Mine." We just wanted to blow away the crowd before the Airplane came on stage. But the minute they set foot onstage we were an afterthought, a speck of dust on the arena floor, because they had the hits and we didn't. They had "White Rabbit" and "Somebody to Love" and they just blew us out of the park. We were out-psychedelicized.

### FRANK ZAPPA

One of the first big-time rock 'n' roll shows we got to do outside of Winnipeg with the Guess Who was in late 1968 at the Retinal Circus in Vancouver with Frank Zappa and the Mothers of Invention and Alice Cooper. We toured with these guys in Seattle, Portland, and San Francisco. I had my 1959 Les Paul by then and Frank Zappa was in love with it. It was such a rare guitar and had a great sound. He tried to buy it from me every night; he loved Gibsons. I let him play it at sound checks, but I'd never sell it to him. I had no idea at the time how rare that guitar was, nor could I have known it would become the "American Woman" guitar.

Frank's band was a collection of jazz musicians, really motley looking guys, and he led them all like an orchestra conductor. He wrote all his music out on charts and gave them to these guys to play. And they would all watch him like a hawk all night because he could change things up at any moment. He'd run around waving his arms and his hands like a symphony conductor. He was quite an amazing guy. He was like a modern-day symphonic composer and conductor, a real genius who elevated the music to a whole new level.

He was also goofy. He named his kids Dweezil and Moon Unit—it's like calling your kid Meatloaf. Actually, I remember walking into the dressing room on New Year's Eve at a gig and Meatloaf was sitting there in his underwear. I said, "Hi, Meat!" and he replied, "Hi." What else are you going to call him? Mr. Loaf? So I guess if you met Moon Unit Zappa you'd say, "Hi, Moon!" Frank was a totally straight guy like me. No drugs, no drinking, no smoking. Just music.

Just last year (2010) I played the High Voltage Festival in London, England, and met Dweezil Zappa there. I told him some stories about his dad. Dwee is a great guitar player and is carrying on the tradition of his dad's musical legacy with a show entitled "Zappa Plays Zappa." It's amazing music.

### VAN MORRISON

When we played around Toronto or southern Ontario, we used to get asked to cross the border and do television shows there. There was a show called *Upbeat* out of Cleveland and we did that a few times. It was kind of like *American Bandstand,* with kids dancing. So, early in 1968, we were there doing the show with Van Morrison. We were over the moon because we loved "Van the Man" from the days of Them and "Baby Please Don't Go," "Gloria," and "Here Comes the Night." We'd done all those songs in our sets.

We approached his dressing room, star-struck, only to find him almost in tears. We went inside and there was the one and only Van Morrison with his head down, looking really dejected.

Randy wearing an old, discarded Union Jack flag to look cool while opening the show at Winnipeg Arena for Jefferson Airplane in 1967. Randy didn't know that the next day was Remembrance Day and the photo became fodder for the newspapers, which claimed that an alderman's son had desecrated the flag.

Randy and his Rickenbacker guitar with the Guess Who at Winnipeg's Polo Park shopping mall, spring 1965.

LEFT: Chet Atkins giving Randy a Gretsch Chet Atkins Super Axe in Vancouver, 1978, as consolation for the theft of Randy's orange 6120 Gretsch in Toronto.

BELOW: Lenny Breau playing a seven-string Kirk Sand guitar.

Randy and Little Richard in 1976 at L.A.'s Van Nuys Sound City Studios, playing on the "Take It Like a Man" and "Stay Alive" tracks for BTO's *Head On* album.

LEFT: The Guess Who receiving a gold record on *American Bandstand* for "These Eyes" in August 1969. Left to right: Garry Peterson, Burton Cummings, Randy Bachman, and Jim Kale.

BELOW: BTO receiving gold records in Germany while on tour in 1976. Left to right: Fred Turner, unknown, Robbie Bachman, Blair Thornton, Bruce Allen (manager), John Austin (road manager), and Randy Bachman.

ABOVE: *Brave Belt II* album cover. Taken in 1972 at the Seven Oaks House museum on the Red River, West Kildonan. Left to right: Fred Turner, Rob Bachman, and Randy Bachman.

RIGHT: BTO rock the PNE Gardens in Vancouver, 1975.

ABOVE: Neil Young and Randy at the "Shakin' All Over: Bands and Fans Reunion" in Winnipeg, celebrating the book *Shakin' All Over* by John Einarson.

RIGHT: Randy and Neil Young at the 2011 Juno Awards. Randy presented the Artist of the Year award to Neil.

TOP: Randy and Rick Mercer on the *Mercer Report*, CBC-TV, 2008.

ABOVE: Randy and Hank Marvin of the Shadows with the famous fiesta-red 1956 Stratocaster, played on every Shadows recording and live show.

RIGHT: Randy and the Bee Gees' Robin Gibb at the ASCAP Music Awards, London, 2009.

LEFT: Randy with Ringo Starr on the ten-month-long Ringo Starr's All-Starrs World Tour, 1995.

BELOW: Randy and his 1965 Thunderbird, which he bought from Burton Cummings in early 2002 and donated to the Canadian Museum of Science and Technology in 2011. This is the last picture of Randy with the car as he drives it to the B.C. ferry for shipping to Ottawa.

RIGHT: Randy and Denise at the Canadian Consulate in L.A., 2010.

BELOW: Randy recording *Vinyl Tap* at CBC studios in Vancouver, 2009.

We asked him what was wrong and he said he had the #1 song in the country, "Brown-Eyed Girl," but he had no money because of a bad contract he'd signed with his record label. On top of that he had no luggage because the airline had lost it, including his guitar. So he couldn't even go out and lip-synch to his big hit. At the time I had an endorsement deal with Yamaha back in Winnipeg to play their guitars, so I had a couple of them with me. I gave him one of my Yamahas. I actually have a video at home of Van lip-synching to "Brown-Eyed Girl" on *Upbeat* with that Yamaha guitar. He wanted to give it back after the show, but I said, "Keep it." He was very pleased. He was going from there to New York. He probably had no idea who we were.

Years later, Denise and I saw Van Morrison perform at Hampton Court Palace in the U.K. It looked like a medieval palace, and inside the castle court they have bleachers and chairs set up. We waited, and sure enough he did "Brown-Eyed Girl" at the end of the show. "Sha la la la la la la." I borrowed that little bit of scat singing for the end of "You Ain't Seen Nothing Yet" and "Hey You."

Musicians will generally help each other out. I remember the time the Stampeders lent the Guess Who a helping hand.

I've known the guys in the Stampeders for many, many years and have played a number of shows with them. They formed in Calgary and took their name from the annual Calgary Stampede. The group was a six-piece before moving to Toronto in the late 60s, where they trimmed down to a trio: Rich Dodson, Ronnie King, and Kim Burly. The Stampeders enjoyed a string of Canadian hit singles in the late 60s to early 70s, including "Sweet City Woman," which went on to become a U.S. hit as well.

The Guess Who were booked to play with the Stampeders somewhere near Niagara Falls, Ontario. We were coming back from the States and crossed the border without any problems, but our equipment truck was held up and searched. We didn't know until we got to the gig that we had no equipment. This was in the years before cell phones. So the Stampeders are up onstage rocking the place, and as their set ends Rich Dodson announces, "Thanks everyone. Now here's the Guess Who!" So we walked out onstage with no instruments or amplifiers. I told Rich what had happened and he took off his guitar and handed it to me. Then Ronnie handed over his bass and we proceeded to play using their gear. The problem for me was that Rich Dodson played a big double-neck guitar like Jimmy Page in Led Zeppelin—a six-string and a twelve-string—and it was so heavy that my shoulder hurt throughout the set. But we made it through thanks to our friends the Stampeders.

### MOE KAUFMAN AND HAGOOD HARDY

In the 1960s, radio was great because the hit parade was very eclectic. You could have the Beatles' latest record followed by Frank Sinatra, Simon & Garfunkel, Bobby Goldsboro, the Doors, and the Tijuana Brass. It wasn't "narrowcasting" to a specific demographic like it is today. It was all just music. It was the same with the players in town: jazz and country guys mixed with rock 'n' rollers.

When we went to Toronto in the fall of 1967 to record in a proper studio, we encountered a bunch of musicians, big studio cats and CBC players, who were classically trained. Plus they were all serious jazz musicians. Here we were, a bunch of prairie punks, rock 'n' roll kids. Even though we'd had music lessons as kids—Burton Cummings has grade 12 piano, I had grade 7 or 8 violin, Garry Peterson had been taking drum lessons since he was three and had played in the Winnipeg Junior Symphony—we were kind of ostracized from these players. They were elitists and we were hicks. But two of those guys did become friendly, and talked with us like we were "cats" just like them. One of these guys was Hagood Hardy; the other was Moe Kaufman of "Swingin' Shepherd Blues" fame. That was a very cool song, basically just a blues song on flute. Moe was a very sweet guy. I remember, as a kid seeing him on TV playing three saxes at the same time.

When Hagood Hardy introduced himself to us, Burton and I said, "Wow, is that your real name?" We used to collect odd names. We'd be in hotels in some city or town late at night after the TV had gone off air, and we'd read through the phone book for weird-sounding names. Hagood told us that his name was real and explained its origin.

We came home after the sessions and then got asked to do an album with Jack Richardson, who'd produced the earlier sessions in Toronto. Burton and I both wrote a song about Hagood Hardy. Burton's was better than mine, so when we went back to Toronto we recorded it. The chorus went, "Heygoode Hardy." That appeared on an album called *A Wild Pair*, which was one side by us, all original material, and the other side by Ottawa's Staccatos, who later became the Five Man Electrical Band. But we became friends with Hagood Hardy, and every time we went to Toronto we'd hang out with him and Moe Kaufman. Who knows, maybe in their younger years they played rock 'n' roll, so they were able to relate to us.

Hagood went on to write and record his own music. He wrote a commercial for Salada Tea called "The Homecoming" that went on to become the theme of a movie of the same name and a big hit. I was at the Juno Awards in the mid 70s when BTO were winning all sorts of awards, and it was really cool to see Hagood also winning awards for his own songwriting.

## CHET ATKINS

When the Guess Who recorded our *Wheatfield Soul* album in New York and signed with RCA, the label had this thing they did, and I'm sure all the record labels did this in the 60s. They would sit you down and ask you a bunch of questions, likes and dislikes, favourite this and that. All sorts of questions like that for their promo bios they would put together and send out to radio stations or teen magazines. "What's your favourite colour? What's your favourite food? Your favourite car? Who are your musical influences?" That kind of stuff.

It was 1968, and so most guys would say their musical influences were Eric Clapton, Jimi Hendrix, the Beatles, or the Stones. But when it came time for my question-and-answer session and I was asked who my musical influences were, I replied, "Hank B. Marvin, Lenny Breau, and Chet Atkins." Lo and behold, who should I meet soon after in the RCA building but the man himself, Chet Atkins, who thanked me for mentioning his name in my bio. He was an executive with RCA and so he knew about our signing with the label. I said that it was an honour to meet him, that I wouldn't be the guitar player I was without having learned from his records and from Lenny Breau, and that I even had a Gretsch Chet Atkins 6120 guitar like his. We also talked about Lenny Breau, since Chet had already heard Lenny play.

Back in Winnipeg I'd sort of become the go-to guy for other guitar players who wanted to learn to play Chet Atkins–style. I'd learned it from spending almost every day at Lenny's house watching him. But Lenny was too busy to teach anyone, so I would take what I learned from him and teach other guys. I had five or six students who used to come to my house on Luxton Avenue one at a time and take lessons. But my biggest regret was lending these guitar players my Chet Atkins albums because I never got them all back. They were gone and were all out of print by then. This was long before CDs. So I mentioned that to Chet in passing, then thanked him for meeting me and influencing me, and went home. That was it.

Not long after that, packages started arriving, one a week for months and months. They were Chet Atkins albums from all over the world. Brand new, still sealed in shrink wrap. He'd gotten every one of his albums where he could find them around the world through RCA's various distributors and sent them to me. I still have them, all unopened, still sealed. Forty or fifty albums. He's a great guy and truly the country gentleman.

When my original orange Gretsch 6120 guitar was stolen in Toronto in the mid 70s and I was desperate to find it, I got a call from Chet Atkins asking me if it was the same guitar I'd shown him years before. I told him it was. He asked for my address and a few weeks later a Gretsch "Atkins Axe Special" model arrived at my house. What a generous man! A few weeks after that, Chet was playing a concert with the Vancouver Symphony and I took the guitar down to the show and had photos taken of him and me with that guitar. He was a very special man.

### GORDON LIGHTFOOT

Sometime in the fall of 1967 the Guess Who were playing Montreal and we had a night off. It was a Tuesday night, and we heard that Gordon Lightfoot was playing a small club. We'd seen him once before at the Riverboat club in Toronto, but this was a bit more intimate. So Burton Cummings and I were there at a table in this tiny club when Lightfoot comes out. There was hardly anyone in the audience because it was a Tuesday night. He was backed by Red Shea on guitar and John Stockfish on bass, just the three of them, and they proceeded to play three solid hours of original material, like "Pussy Willows Cattails," "Canadian Railroad Trilogy," "Did She Mention My Name," "Early Morning Rain"—all his great songs. Burton and I sat there, stunned. The most amazing songs and incredible lyrics, hit after hit and non-hit album tracks, too. We just looked at each other and said, "Wow. If this guy from Orillia can write this many great original songs, we can certainly write our own original songs."

That experience prompted Burton and me to go home to Winnipeg and start writing the songs that became the hits for the Guess Who and made us such a successful songwriting team. We even wrote a song about Gordon called "Lightfoot." But the inspiration came from Canada's greatest songwriter, Gordon Lightfoot.

## JUNIOR WALKER AND THE ALL STARS

In late 1969, Junior Walker and the All Stars, a Motown group, recorded a soulful cover version of "These Eyes," adding a lot of saxophone and a whole new texture to our song. And besides giving a great R&B feel to the song, it actually saved Burton and me from a likely beating or worse. We were in Chicago for a gig, and afterwards I went to collect the money. As usual I had a bagful of small bills, three or four thousand dollars in ones, fives, and tens. I always figured it was safer carrying it in a grocery bag because it was less conspicuous than an attaché case. Those were like a neon sign saying "Money." At about three in the morning, I got a phone call in my hotel room that Burton needed to be picked up somewhere. So I picked him up in the station wagon we'd rented. The bag of money had been stuffed under the seat until I could get to a bank the next morning.

I got lost on the way back to our hotel. We were in the black part of town. People were out in the streets drinking and partying, doors open, music blaring out. I drove around for a while and realized we were the only white people in the area. Being innocent Canadians, Burton and I entered a juke joint to ask directions back to the hotel. There was a party going on as we entered and sought out the bartender. Before we could locate him, though, several large black gentlemen accosted us.

"What are you doing here, Whitey?!"

Realizing we were in the wrong place, we tried to back out but were immediately encircled. Suddenly Junior Walker's version of "These Eyes" came on the jukebox.

"What are you guys doing in here?!"

"We're lost," I stammered. "We're the Guess Who from Canada. We wrote that song."

"No, you didn't. Man, that's a black group."

"No, really, we wrote it." At that point one guy goes over to the jukebox and looks at the record label.

"What's your name?" he asks.

"Randy Bachman."

"And what's your name?" he turned to Burton and asked.

"Burton Cummings."

He looked at the label again.

"You wrote that song for Junior? Do you know Junior Walker?!"

"Yes," we replied in unison, terrified.

"Okay, well, you go out here, turn right, go down Cicero and that'll get you back downtown."

We thanked them and beat a hasty retreat, managing to find our way back to our hotel. Thank you, Junior Walker.

### STEVE CROPPER

Our album *Wheatfield Soul* was out, "These Eyes" was a hit, and we were still on the radio with "Laughing" and "Undun." Junior Walker's version of "These Eyes" was out and we were booked to play in Memphis, Tennessee. The other guys were seriously getting into partying by then, but I'd get up in the mornings and do things. When we arrived in Memphis we passed the famous Stax-Volt studios on the way to the hotel. It looked more like a restaurant or grocery store than a recording studio. In fact, it had once been a movie house because it still had that marquee sign out front that said "Stax" in big black letters. So I asked the guys if they wanted to go with me the following day to visit the studio. They weren't interested, so the next morning I got up early to take care of the deposit from the night before and decided to try visiting Stax-Volt studios.

It was ten in the morning, so I phoned the studio, told them who I was and mentioned some of our hits, and received an invitation to come by. When I got there the front door was locked; it was too early. I peeked through the round windows into the lobby of the theatre, now a studio, and saw a janitor sweeping up. I introduced myself and he let me in. He told me his name: Rufus Thomas. It was a Saturday so I figured nothing would be going on, but I asked if I could look around anyway. He said sure, then told me that there was a session starting in about an hour with Booker T. and the MGs. I thought, "Wow! 'Green Onions' and all those great instrumentals." The guitar player in the MGs was Steve Cropper and I loved his playing.

Steve Cropper arrived not long after and introduced himself. He knew of our records and asked me about some of the chords in "These Eyes." He wasn't familiar with some of the major seventh chords we'd used. So here I am showing the one and only Steve Cropper the chords for "These Eyes." That was an experience I'll never forget. He expressed interest in recording "A Wednesday in Your Garden" with the Staple Singers. I was thrilled with that. He was the man behind the funky Memphis soul sound of Booker T. and the MGs, Sam and Dave, Otis Redding, and so many more. Steve Cropper is a unique guitar player with an immediately identifiable sound that has influenced everyone from Pete Townshend to rock/jazz fusion guitarist Jeff Beck, and me, too.

## CHUCK BERRY AND JERRY LEE LEWIS

It was July 27, 1969, outside of Seattle in Woodinville, Washington. It was called the Seattle Pop Festival and I was with the Guess Who. "These Eyes" had already been a gold record and "Laughing" was on its way to the same. We hadn't recorded "American Woman" yet. The Seattle Pop Festival was three glorious days of sunshine and music, way, way better than Woodstock, but it wasn't filmed like Woodstock was. On the bill were the Byrds, the Flying Burrito Brothers, Ten Years After, the Doors, Ike and Tina Turner, Led Zeppelin, Santana, Bo Diddley, us, and many more. It was an amazing weekend that I'll never forget.

We did more festivals down the West Coast, and at one of them the founding fathers of rock 'n' roll were booked to perform: Chuck Berry and Jerry Lee Lewis. On the afternoon of the final day, two Cadillacs pull up backstage. Chuck Berry is in one and Jerry Lee Lewis in the other. The doors to these Cadillacs are wide open and the two start drinking. In those days the headliner appeared last, so they start arguing back and forth from their Cadillacs over who's going to close the show. Each is claiming to be the father of rock 'n' roll. They're arguing back and forth, and then their managers start arguing with each other. It's crazy.

Finally they decide to flip a coin. Jerry Lee Lewis loses the coin toss, so Chuck Berry will close the show. The implication was that Chuck, not Jerry Lee, was the king of rock 'n' roll. So the time comes for Jerry Lee to go onstage and he just goes crazy, pounding the keys of the grand piano like a wild man with his hair flying around. He's playing like crazy. Then, while his band plays on, he goes offstage and comes back with an axe and starts chopping the piano up. Splinters of wood and ivory are flying everywhere. He then pulls out a cigarette lighter and lighter fluid and proceeds to set the remains of the piano on fire. The crowd is going insane by this point. Before he walks offstage, Jerry Lee walks up to the microphone and says: "Nobody follows the Killer." True to those words, Chuck Berry gets in his Cadillac and drives away without performing. Who could follow that anyway?

### JOHN FOGERTY

In late 1969, the Guess Who played with Creedence Clearwater Revival at the Los Angeles Forum at a sold-out show. In the Top 10 in L.A. that week Creedence had four songs and the Guess Who had three. How amazing was that?! The two bands rocked the Forum that night.

In the dressing room before the show, I was noodling around playing my jazzy Lenny Breau licks. John Fogerty heard me playing and said, "Very cool stuff. Just don't play it on your records." I've always remembered that. I always play a solo a fourteen-year-old kid thinks he can play when he hears it on the radio. He'll go out and buy the record and learn it. If it's all this weird complicated stuff, something way out or jazzy, he'll never buy that record. I always sing a solo first and then I play it. I make my solos very melodic. If someone else can sing it, they can play it. I always think about that when writing and recording.

Lenny Breau taught me that the spaces are as important as the notes in a solo. Leave some holes and make people anticipate the next note. B.B. King told me that, too. What I learned from Lenny was a playing etiquette—not to go berserk with a barrage of notes. I took that approach on my *JazzThing* album.

## ᴄℳy Picks

"BE-BOP-A-LULA" by Gene Vincent and the Blue Caps

"BORIS THE SPIDER" by the Who (featuring John Entwistle)

"BROWN-EYED GIRL" by Van Morrison

"CALL ANY VEGETABLE" by the Mothers of Invention

"CROSSFIRE" by Johnny and the Hurricanes

"DA DO RON RON" by the Crystals

"EARLY MORNING RAIN" by Gordon Lightfoot

"FORTUNATE SON" by Creedence Clearwater Revival

"FORTUNE TELLER" by Bobby Curtola

"GREAT BALLS OF FIRE" by Jerry Lee Lewis

"HEYGOODE HARDY" by the Guess Who

"HITCH HIKER" by Bobby Curtola

"HOW HIGH THE MOON" by Les Paul and Mary Ford

"JOHNNY B. GOODE" by Chuck Berry

"LET IT RIDE" by BTO

"LIGHTFOOT" by the Guess Who

"LOTTA LOVIN'" by Gene Vincent and the Blue Caps

"OH BY JINGO" by Chet Atkins

"RED RIVER ROCK" by Johnny and the Hurricanes

"RUNAROUND SUE" by Dion and the Belmonts

"STONE FREE" by Jimi Hendrix

"SUMMERTIME" by Randy Bachman with Lenny Breau

"SWINGIN' SHEPHERD BLUES" by Moe Kaufman

"TAKING CARE OF BUSINESS" by BTO

"THESE EYES" by Junior Walker and the All Stars

"A WEDNESDAY IN YOUR GARDEN" by the Staple Singers

"WHEN FRIENDS FALL OUT" by the Guess Who

"WHITE RABBIT" by Jefferson Airplane

"WILD EYES" by the Stampeders

"YOU AIN'T SEEN NOTHING YET" by BTO

# Shadows and Reflections

The first time I heard the distinctive melodic instrumental music of the Shadows I was instantly smitten. It was the beginning of a lifelong admiration for the group's intricate, guitar-driven sound. The U.K. quartet became my mentors, with Shadows lead guitarist Hank Marvin serving as my very own hero.

The story of how I fell in love with the Shadows starts with how I joined Allan and the Silvertones. Allan and the Silvertones were a popular group from the other side of the Red River in East Kildonan whose reputation had spread around the city. I first heard about them in around 1961. They needed a rhythm guitar player because the guy they had, Johnny Glowa, had quit to go back to school. He'd even sold his orange Gretsch 6120 guitar to Neil Young. So I was asked to audition on rhythm guitar; I guess they knew of me from the Velvetones. Allan Kowbel was playing lead guitar at the time. The group's repertoire consisted largely of material from England's Cliff Richard and the Shadows, whose guitar player was Hank Marvin. I'd never heard the Shadows until I met Allan. He gave me a couple of their EPs to learn from, which, I think, had "Kon Tiki," "Man of Mystery," "FBI," and songs like that. They gave me a few days to learn the songs before my audition. Learning the chords was no problem, and the melodies were a piece of cake for me, so I learned them too just for fun. With my background in melody from years of violin, moving on to the Shadows seemed natural.

Featuring Hank Marvin on lead guitar, Bruce Welch on rhythm guitar, drummer Tony Meehan (replaced by Brian Bennett), and Jet Harris on bass, the Shadows initially came together in 1958 as backing group for U.K. pop sensation Cliff Richard. Dubbed England's very own Elvis Presley, Cliff recorded and toured with the Shadows, whose two guitars, bass, and drums lineup became the template for British rock bands, including the Beatles. Beginning in 1960 with "Apache," the Shadows carved out a separate career recording instrumentals, going on to score thirty-five chart hits on their own as well as charting almost as many times with Cliff Richard, making them the third most successful singles recording act in U.K. music history.

With his trademark Buddy Holly glasses and fiesta-red Fender Stratocaster (reputed to be the first Stratocaster in the U.K.), Hank Marvin became an inspiration to thousands of British teens who picked up guitars in the wake of their success. Hank's use of an echo effect and his vibrato arm on his guitar were integral to his sound. He'd seen James Burton playing a Fender Telecaster backing Ricky Nelson, and so, with no Fender dealers in the U.K. in 1959 and not knowing what else to do, he wrote away to Fender in California and sent money for a Telecaster. But what they sent him was a Stratocaster like the one Buddy Holly played and later Jimi Hendrix. Hank played it on every Shadows recording and on every record they made with Cliff Richard. Hank's fiesta-red Stratocaster is legendary.

At the next Silvertones rehearsal Allan was playing lead guitar and singing, with me just playing the chords for rhythm. In the middle of a song he broke a string, and so I immediately switched from rhythm to lead and finished the song. When it was done I thought that was it for me; I had stepped on his toes. The guys were all looking at me when Allan said, "It's so hard to play lead and sing at the same time. I'll just play rhythm. Randy, you're now the lead guitar player." That was it. I was in the Silvertones. Since we patterned ourselves after the Shadows, we changed our name to the Reflections. Chad Allan was our Cliff Richard and we were like his Shadows.

Our piano player, Bob Ashley, had an old German Korting tape recorder, and he mentioned that if you turn the heads out—one is record and the other play—you could get an echo effect. Hank Marvin used an Echoplex in the Shadows. We didn't know what an Echoplex was; you couldn't buy one in Winnipeg back then. I begged and pleaded with Ashley and finally he let me use it. I had special patch cords made, and plugged my Gretsch guitar into his tape recorder and from that into Jim Kale's Fender Concert amp. I got the most incredible echo sound from that little homemade system. That became *my* sound. I remember Neil Young raving about my having a homemade Echoplex and sounding just like Hank.

I was so taken with the Shadows sound that I wrote my own Hank Marvin–style instrumental. I called it "Made in England." We recorded it in early 1964 at Kay Bank studio in Minneapolis. I was so naive that I even sent a copy of "Made in England" to the Shadows in London. I thought it was good enough for them to record. Duh! I got a rejection letter in the mail on the group's own letterhead, four guys in silhouette, saying, "We received your record but unfortunately we do not feel it is appropriate to record at this time." I still have the letter.

### "SPRING IS NEARLY HERE"

In the 1990s I heard that Sting was organizing a tribute album to the Shadows and Hank Marvin on his own record label, so I sent his management a fax. In the fax I said, "I grew up with Neil Young, and Hank Marvin was our greatest influence. Neil Young went on to find fame with the Buffalo Springfield, Crosby, Stills, Nash and Young, and on his own. I was a member of the

Guess Who and Bachman-Turner Overdrive. Most of our solos are Hank Marvin–inspired. I would love to do a track on the album and I will try to talk Neil into it as well." I received a reply fax the next day saying they'd love to have me and if possible Neil, too, on the album since we were such huge Hank Marvin fans. All these great guitar players like Brian May from Queen, Peter Frampton, Keith Urban, Mark Knopfler from Dire Straits, and Peter Green were going to be on it playing their favourite Shadows song. But the tracks had pretty much been recorded already; I'd heard about the project late. I was told there was room for one more track. All the good songs like "Wonderful Land," "Man of Mystery," "Nivram," and "FBI" were already taken. I didn't know what to pick.

I faxed Neil to tell him about the album and he was onside right away. We fixed a date for me to come down to his Broken Arrow ranch in northern California to record. But record what? Before I left, Neil and I talked on the phone about which song we would do.

"Do you remember 'Spring Is Nearly Here'?" he asked me. "I'd like to play that."

"Yeah," I replied, "Doc Steen used to play it on CKRC back in the 60s."

The problem was that I couldn't find that song on *any* of my Shadows albums, and I pretty much had every Shadows album released in Canada. If we did try that song it would have to be from memory. So off I went to Neil's place. I even played a white 1964 Burns model guitar like Hank played in his latter years with the Shadows. I wanted to be authentic. I showed up with that at Neil's place and he freaked out.

Since neither of us had a recording of the song, we had to try and do it by memory. Neil closed his eyes and a few seconds later he started playing the melody. He hadn't heard the song since 1963 and never had the record. But as soon as he played the opening riff I suddenly remembered the song: "Oh yeah!" I joined in on the rhythm and we got through the verses. Then Neil stopped and said, "I forget the bridge."

"It's in C, so I'll go to a C7 chord and then to F." Shadows songs were pretty predictable. We went through it again, and as I hit the C7, Neil went right into the original bridge. We were pulling these notes from each other's brains. So we had the verse and chorus, but we were still stuck for the intro and outro. We decided to make up an intro that we both liked. "Hank Marvin's not going to care," Neil said.

We finished the recording in one or two takes. Neil likes things to be in the moment. He never likes to do take after take after take or to overdub. There were a couple of odd notes that I thought we should fix, but Neil said, "No! It happened. Pretend we're the Shadows playing live at some seaside resort in Brighton just like in those Cliff Richard movies." So I left it alone and figured I'd fix them once I was back in my own studio in Vancouver.

The next day before I left, Elliot Roberts, Neil's long-time manager, took me aside and said, "We know you have plans to take the tape of 'Spring Is Nearly Here' home and fix it up, but Neil feels strongly that this was a moment captured in time and nothing should alter it." So I didn't. I left the mistake and sent the tape to Sting's manager, who later told me Sting loved the track and said we sounded like the Shadows live.

But I couldn't shake the thought that maybe it wasn't a Shadows song we'd recorded after all. I hadn't been able to find the song on any Shadows albums. Did they actually record "Spring Is Nearly Here"? Did Neil and I remember it correctly or had we recorded a Santo and Johnny song by mistake? So I called a Shadows expert, Richard Patterson, who'd been the drummer in an Ottawa Shadows-style band, the Esquires, back in the mid 60s, and left a frantic message on his answering machine.

"Richard, you have to help me. I can't find a Shadows song called 'Spring Is Nearly Here' anywhere! Can you help me? Do you know that song?"

I took my teenage daughter Callianne to school, and as I walked back into the house I heard "Spring Is Nearly Here" coming from my answering machine. Richard had found the track! It turned out to be on a British album not released in Canada, and we pretty much had it right, pulling it from our collective memories.

The tribute album was called *Twang*, and when it came out it was great, but it was also obvious that none of us, all these great guitar players, could match Hank Marvin's sound. Although we all tried, there's only one Hank Marvin. We were all just imitators.

### THE SHADOWS' REUNION

Despite my lifelong infatuation with the Shadows in general and Hank Marvin in particular, I'd never seen the band performing live. In their heyday they hadn't toured Canada and had broken up by 1990. In 2005 it was announced that the group was re-forming for a farewell tour of U.K. and European concert dates. I was not about to miss my one and only opportunity to catch my heroes live.

As soon as I heard about the farewell tour I emailed a friend in the U.K. and said, "Please, whatever you have to do, I need tickets to the Shadows' farewell show. If you have to camp out to get them, please do so. Don't worry about the cost; I'll pay any price. I'll even pay you to stand in line. I *have* to see the Shadows." I rearranged my schedule to be in London a week earlier so that I could attend the show. I got four tickets and invited Neil and his wife, Pegi Young. They were all set to go, but then their son Ben had a minor accident, nothing serious, but Neil emailed me to say he couldn't go. I ended up telling him all about the concert when we hooked up later that year. He wanted to know all the details and what songs they played.

My friend had contacted the Shadows' manager, who arranged for me to go to their sound check that afternoon and meet them before the show. I had briefly met Bruce Welch before, at a banquet for U.K. songwriters called SODS, the Society of Distinguished Songwriters, but not all the other guys in the band. When I went to the sound check I gave them a message from Neil who couldn't be there and introduced myself. Bruce, Hank, and Brian Bennett were there. I'd brought my very rare 1964 Burns-model white Hank Marvin guitar with me. I took the pick guard off it and got it signed.

I'd bought some old Vox amps, Vox AC 30s, like the Shadows used to use. One had "Hank Marvin—The Shadows" stencilled on the back. It had been one of Hank's original Vox amplifiers. So I brought the back of his amp with me along with a *Shadows 20 Greatest Hits* gold record award I'd bought off the internet. Being the consummate Shadows fan, I brought all this stuff with me to the sound check.

When they finished sound-checking they jumped off the front of the stage and came over and shook hands with me. Denise took a bunch of pictures and I said to them, "I'm a silly fan … would you please sign these?" Hey, I'm just a guy from Winnipeg. They signed the gold record, the pick guard, and the back of the amp. I was ecstatic. I'm a huge fan and love those guys.

Now I have my Shadows shrine in my house.

They were so sweet and wonderful to me, and talked to me like we were old friends. When it comes right down to it we're all musicians and normal guys, but in my mind I'm thinking these are the greatest guys in the world. I mean, I used to dream of meeting and playing with the Shadows one day. I knew all their songs, and told them how I got the gig with Chad Allan when he broke a string playing a Shadows song and I soared right into the lead without missing a beat. And how the lead lick in "You Ain't Seen Nothing Yet" is basically the Shadows' "Wonderful Land" played inverted with an echo. They thought this was all fantastic. For me, it was like meeting Elvis. These guys were my original heroes. What was amazing, too, for me was that they knew my music and knew who I was.

Then Hank Marvin said to me, "Do you want to play my guitar?"

"What?!"

So he took me up onstage and handed me his fiesta-red Stratocaster that he's famous for, the Hank Marvin guitar.

"Here, go ahead," Hank said. "Play it."

Denise took a picture of me holding Hank's beloved Stratocaster. I was so nervous I didn't know what to play, so I didn't play anything. How do you play a Shadows song in front of Hank Marvin?

That night at the concert as they played all those great songs, I had tears streaming down my cheeks. My daughter Callianne couldn't understand why I was crying. I was seeing my heroes. Every great guitar player in the U.K. was in the audience and they, too, were feeling the same emotions. After the show I went to their dressing room and gave them all hugs and handshakes. It was the most wonderful feeling in my life meeting these guys.

### POSTSCRIPT

In 2007 Burton Cummings and I entered a Toronto recording studio to lay down covers of some of our most cherished songs from our youth. It was a pet project motivated more by fun than anything else. Among the seventeen tracks on *Jukebox* is a version of the Shadows' "Man of Mystery." We also tackled Cliff Richard and the Shadows' "Don't Talk to Him," with Burton sounding very much like Cliff.

In the original recording of "Man of Mystery" there was a little mistake where the band played a minor chord and Hank went to a major chord. I corrected it in our recording. When I gave that version to Bruce Welch and Brian Bennett I told them I'd corrected the mistake Hank made on the original, and they replied, "Oh, thank god! We argued and argued with Hank at the time about that mistake, but he just said that was the one take, so it just stayed there."

## *My Picks*

"APACHE" by the Shadows

"DON'T TALK TO HIM" by Bachman and Cummings

"FBI" by the Shadows

"MADE IN ENGLAND" by Chad Allan and the Reflections

"MAN OF MYSTERY" by Bachman and Cummings

"ON THE BEACH" by Cliff Richard and the Shadows

"THE RISE AND FALL OF FLINGEL BUNT" by the Shadows

"SPRING IS NEARLY HERE" by Randy Bachman and Neil Young

"SPRING IS NEARLY HERE" by the Shadows

# The Story Behind the Song, Part 2

When I left the Guess Who in 1970 I wanted to do something different musically. I didn't want to compete with my former band. Brave Belt was my post–Guess Who band, and instead of rock it was a country-rock experiment, an experiment that failed. People still expected me to be that rockin' "American Woman" and "No Time" guy. So I needed to rethink things. Bringing Fred Turner into the band was the key ingredient in the transformation from Brave Belt to Bachman-Turner Overdrive, or BTO. Not only did Fred have a great hard-rock voice but he also wrote songs that suited the way I thought we should be sounding.

### "GIMME YOUR MONEY PLEASE"

We cut our first Bachman-Turner Overdrive album, 1973's *BTO I,* which was pretty much the *Brave Belt III* album, in Toronto. It didn't have any hit singles on it, but it got us a lot of FM radio play. One of the songs on it was written in New York by C.F. "Fred" Turner. We were in New York as Brave Belt and Fred was out for a walk. He turned a corner and there was a guy, with a knife and his hand out, who said to Fred, "Gimme your money, please." Fred gave him his money, came back to his room, and told me about it. It had been pretty terrifying, and he wrote the song about it. That was the song Charlie Fach, head of Mercury Records, was listening to when he called and told me we had a record deal after some twenty rejections. It's a great rockin' song that solidified our image: no-frills blue-collar rockers.

### "BLUE COLLAR"

But the cool thing about our *BTO I* album was that it wasn't all pile-driving rockers. Fred Turner's "Blue Collar" song was a real left turn and went a long way towards earning us respect as something more than heavy-riffing Canucks.

Fred had been walking in Regina really early one morning as the sun was just starting to come up and he saw these guys going to work. They were labour-type workers and they all had blue shirts on with blue collars, your typical labourer shirt. He came back to our hotel and wrote the song about how "you walk your street and I walk mine." I was looking for a song to stretch out on and play some Lenny Breau/Jeff Beck–style jazzy guitar. So along with the ear-splitting, straight-ahead hard rock on *BTO I*, out comes this jazzy song, "Blue Collar." I still have guitar players come up to me today and tell me how great it was in the early 70s in that era of hard rock to hear that song on rock radio.

We didn't use a lot of overdubs on BTO recordings. I wanted our records to sound like four guys playing live, no studio wizardry. We geared our music to the lowest common denominator, basic primal rock 'n' roll. Any embellishments would be noticed only after repeated listening because they were very subtle. We didn't use synthesizers or stacked voices, and if I added bits here and there they were less obvious but still important. For example, on "Blue Collar" I added a low piano bass note at the beginning of each chord that emphasized the chord. You don't hear it as a piano part, but if it wasn't there the chord wouldn't be as strong. It's a subtle but essential ingredient underpinning the structure and presentation.

### "LET IT RIDE"

*BTO I* established us as a strong band and all our touring was paying off. When it came time to record our second album, *BTO II,* in 1974, I started to focus on writing for the singles market. Charlie Fach at Mercury Records had told us that we had the album thing down well and that we should try writing some hit singles. He wanted us to write more commercial songs for the next album because he wanted a hit single. Mercury Records had tried editing some of the songs on *BTO I* down to singles length, but it really hadn't worked. Charlie said people like songs with a verse and chorus that they can all sing along to. So when we recorded *BTO II* that's what we were going for, and we succeeded. We really hit our stride on that album, and we started getting both FM and AM airplay. My focus after that became not extended album tracks but writing commercially good rock songs. I realized that's what I do best.

Between the two albums, we'd been touring constantly. Wherever the album was getting airplay we'd go there. On one occasion we were travelling through Louisiana when a truck cut us off on the highway. We got to the next truck stop and saw the truck parked there. Being polite Canadians, we thought we would tell this guy to watch his driving.

"You cut us off back there on the highway," we told him politely.

He looked straight at us and replied, "Ain't no big deal. Just let it ride, buddy."

We were like a truckers' band anyway, so we decided to write a song using the phrase "Let it ride." We'd been touring with the Doobie Brothers, so the song kind of took on a Doobies' guitar feel.

I based the chords around a guitar pattern that I got from Antonin Dvořák's "Piano Concerto in D." I was trying to be influenced by classical writers the way John Lennon had been. So I listened to Dvořák's "Piano Concerto," which is very boring, but just as when I heard Bob Dylan in "Ballad in Plain D" say "She's come undone," I was about to turn off Dvořák when I heard this melodic pattern. I figured out chords for it, and it became the beginning to "Let It Ride." It's very memorable, like a melody within the chords. From there it went into the ca-chunka chunka heavier part. The song really tricks the listener because it starts mellow then thunders into the rhythm. "Let It Ride" put us on the singles charts and at the forefront of harder rock guitar bands.

The album managed to capture that territory for us with two chart hits and one rock anthem. The melodic chording and sledgehammer verses of "Let It Ride" became the trademark sound of Bachman-Turner Overdrive. BTO was a guys' band. Fred Turner and I didn't look like pretty boys or models. We were the guys next door who took out your garbage, mowed your lawn, or delivered your newspaper. Because of our name and image, we did a lot of truck-driving songs: "Let It Ride," "Roll on Down the Highway," "Four Wheel Drive," "My Wheels Won't Turn."

Here's something most people don't know. BTO's secret weapon on many of our records was a gallon milk jug turned over and played in a galloping style. It simulated that Beatles bongo sound. Robbie played it, and we had two tones, one with the cap off and the other with the cap on. It's that gallop that's in "Let It Ride," "Takin' Care of Business," and lots of other BTO songs mixed under the track to give it that galloping effect, propelling the song along.

### "TAKIN' CARE OF BUSINESS"

This is BTO's signature song and a bona fide rock anthem. Like "American Woman" three years before, "Takin' Care of Business" was born from an impromptu moment on stage and refined into a hit record in the studio. Talk about a song having legs: "Takin' Care of Business" remains the most licensed song in Sony Music's vast publishing catalogue and has been used in everything from movies to selling burgers and office supplies. And it never fails to bring an audience to its feet.

In Winnipeg, you drive to work. There are no commuter trains. When the Guess Who were recording *Wheatfield Soul* in New York in 1968 we stayed at the Gramercy Hotel in Manhattan, and I'd see all these people who worked in New York arriving by commuter train every morning. So I wrote a song I called "White Collar Worker" about all these guys taking the 8:15 into the city every day and going back home at night. And the girls were all trying to look pretty as they came to work each day. I had seen it in movies, a day in the life of your typical New York businessman.

"White Collar Worker" had the same verses as "Takin' Care of Business" played over about seven or eight chord changes. The lyrics had that Chuck Berry "Maybellene" or "Johnny B. Goode" storytelling style to them. The chorus was copied from the Beatles' "Paperback Writer," where we stopped and sang "White collar worker" in harmonies just like the Beatles did. I tried "White Collar Worker" out in my basement on Luxton Avenue with Burton Cummings and Garry Peterson, but it was pretty terrible. They hated it, so the Guess Who never recorded it and I forgot about it.

So fast-forward a couple of years and BTO are playing a club gig in Vancouver. I'm on my way to the gig with my radio on and I hear a deejay on the radio say something like "This is Daryl B. on CFOX radio takin' care of business." I thought that was a cool phrase. That night, Fred Turner blew his voice out after singing three sets a night all week long. By the last set he could barely croak, so he asked me to take over. After singing a few cover songs that I knew, out of desperation I thought of "White Collar Worker." I couldn't shout out all the chord changes since there were so many, so I simplified it in my head and told the guys to play C Bb and F over and over. That allowed me to sing the lyrics in a more Chuck Berry way over a simpler chord progression. When we got to the chorus, I just sang "Takin' care of business" four times over those same three chords. We did another verse and went into the chorus, and out of the blue as the others joined in singing "Takin' care of business," I just answered each one with "Every day," "Every way," "It's all mine," "And working overtime" followed by "Work out."

When we finished the song people kept clapping, stomping, and shouting "Takin' care of business" over and over. So we picked up the tempo a bit and played it again. We knew we had something. After that we played it at other gigs and received the same response from audiences. We started closing our sets with it and the crowds wouldn't let us off the stage.

We couldn't record a song called "White Collar Worker" in BTO when we already had "Blue Collar," so the title was no good. But I knew the verses were great: "They get up in the mornin' from the alarm clock's warnin', take the 8:15 into the city." It's one of those songs you can't help but sing along to.

When we went into Kaye-Smith Studios in Seattle to record *BTO II,* I gave Fred the lyrics to sing it. Instead he said, "I'm not going to sing it. You should sing it. It'll give me a break."

I've never really thought of myself as a singer. What I am is a guitar player who sings. I don't have the greatest singing voice. It's distinctive, though, and over the years I've come to accept that I do have a voice.

In the studio we simplified the chords and tightened up the arrangement. I put the break in the middle to change up the monotony of the three chords over and over. As we were finishing the recording there was a knock at the studio door. I opened it and there stood this guy, six-foot-four, big beard like Fidel Castro, wearing army fatigues and holding a pizza.

"Did you guys order pizza?"

I told him we didn't but that maybe someone else in the building had. So off he went down the hall with his pizza and we went back to listening to the playback of "Takin' Care of Business." It was about one-thirty in the morning. A few minutes later there was another knock at the door. I opened it and there's the pizza guy again.

"That song sounds like it could really use a piano. I'm a piano player. Give me a shot."

It was late and we were ready to call it a night, so I said to him, "Okay, you've got one take."

We played the track for him. He listened and wrote down the chords. Then he went out into the studio, sat down at the piano they had, and laid down this great piano part. One take. Then we all went home.

A few days later we played the song for Charlie Fach from Mercury Records and he flipped out. He loved the piano part and said it gave BTO a whole new sound. But we couldn't release it without paying the piano player and crediting him on the album. So I started going through the Yellow Pages alphabetically, phoning all the pizza joints in town and describing this guy to them.

I finally tracked him down. His name was Norman Durkee and he was a classically trained pianist who worked with the symphony orchestra. In between gigs he delivered pizza. So we got hold of him, paid him double scale, and the song came out and made musical history. And part of its appeal is that piano part. Norman later became the rehearsal pianist for the L.A. Symphony.

I didn't think of "Takin' Care of Business" in terms of being a single, especially with me singing it. It was an album track. Fred Turner was our lead singer. But after "Let It Ride" was a hit and slipping down the charts, Charlie Fach told us he wanted "Takin' Care of Business" to be the next single. It was already getting airplay in some regions. The trouble was I didn't want it to be a single, and I told Charlie that.

"I sang it terribly. It's only an album track."

But I couldn't deny the momentum that was there. "Takin' Care of Business" became a single because of radio demand. More than that, "takin' care of business" was becoming an American catchphrase. It had several meanings, whether for a guy and his girl getting it on or for someone who just wants to get the job done. Everyone knew what it meant. Even Elvis used it as his catchphrase. It fit the band as well, these big Canadian lumberjack guys who take care of business. The song has gone way beyond the record charts and makes more money now than it did back then. But if I'd known that, I would have spent more time on the lyrics and replaced the first part of "If it were easy as fishin', you could be a musician" with "If you pass the audition." Too late now.

### "YOU AIN'T SEEN NOTHING YET"

So there we were. It was 1974 and we were getting ready to lay down tracks for our third album, *Not Fragile*. We had conquered both the albums and singles markets, FM and AM radio. The group was on a roll and about to turn a North American success story into an international phenomenon.

BTO was a bunch of brothers and a friend. Sounds kind of like the Beach Boys. It was all for one and one for all. We had endured the lean years and worked our butts off for the success we achieved.

Our albums had always featured eight songs, four on one side and four on the other, like wheels on a truck. When it came time to record *Not Fragile*, we had our eight songs recorded. But before we started recording the album I had what I called a work song that had a light part to get the rhythm and a heavy riffing part to set the balance. I used it as my testing song to see if we were getting the right balance before we tackled the real songs intended for the album. I was really just fooling around on that song. I took the opening jangly chord from Dave Mason's "Only You Know and I Know" and added some heavy chords on the chorus. As we played it to get ourselves into the recording mindset I started singing words. "I met a devil woman, she took my heart away." I honestly don't know where I got the line "You ain't seen nothing yet" from or why I stuttered on those particular words, but when I did "B-b-b-baby," everybody in the band sat up and got into it.

I figured I would keep it and work on it for a later album. We recorded it, but not with the intention of using it. It was just this silly little ditty and we set it aside.

My older brother Gary had a stuttering problem as a kid. He'd overcome it by the time he was an adult, but I used to tease him when we were kids growing up in Winnipeg. So as a joke I thought I would finish up the track and send it to him. Nothing more than that.

But I never did send it to Gary. When Charlie Fach came out to Seattle to hear the tracks for our third album he was concerned that while the album tracks were great, there was no obvious single that he heard. There was no "Let It Ride" or "Takin' Care of Business." Our engineer, Mark Smith, suggested we play Charlie my stuttering song. The minute he heard those intro chords, he yelled, "This is a radio hit!"

Then the stuttering vocals came in and I started to cringe.

"You've got to put this on the album!" Charlie insisted. "It's a monster!"

The recording was full of stammers and stutters, all kinds of goofing around, and had a slightly out-of-tune guitar. But Charlie said it had magic in the tracks. He was the man who'd discovered "Hey Baby" for Bruce Channel and "Maggie May" for Rod Stewart. You can't argue with that. So he said to put it on the album the way it was. I thought it would be the end of the band, but Charlie's instincts were right.

Before we released the album I tried to re-record "You Ain't Seen Nothing Yet" with a better vocal and a guitar riff that was in tune, but nothing worked. So I was forced to leave it as is.

When the album came out, it was "You Ain't Seen Nothing Yet" that got the most airplay, so Charlie insisted it be released as the first single off *Not Fragile.*

"No way! I do not want this as a single."

I heard it on the radio one day and was so embarrassed I turned it off. I just figured people would hear how bad the vocal was and my slightly out-of-tune guitar. I was wrong. People loved that song and still do. It went to #1 in some twenty or so countries in 1974 and into 1975. We got gold records from places like Germany and Turkey. We rode that song for two years. It became BTO's only million-selling single.

### "HEY YOU"

BTO's success was sweet. *Not Fragile* sold over two million copies and hit #1 on the Billboard album charts while "You Ain't Seen Nothing Yet" topped singles charts worldwide. Everything we touched turned to gold. But I wasn't looking to rub it in anyone's face. The music and the success spoke for themselves. And I did feel some satisfaction knowing that our hard work had paid off. I think I also dispelled the myth in the music business that you couldn't make it straight, drug-free. I was told when I left the Guess Who that I'd never make it in this business straight. I also showed Burton Cummings and company that I was still a force in music and couldn't be put down anymore.

So in "Hey You" there are some references to Burton and the Guess Who. When we played that song in recent years in our Bachman-Cummings shows, Burton introduces "Hey You" as a song written "when Randy wasn't happy with me." I wrote it after "You Ain't Seen Nothing Yet" and *Not Fragile* both hit #1. "You say you want to change the world, it's all right, with me there's no regrets. It's my turn, the circle game has brought me here." It was my turn to be on top. I certainly felt that way after reaching #1 again with a band that I had basically salvaged from nothing. We weren't any better players than the guys in the Guess Who, but we'd worked hard to get where we were against a lot of odds and in a much shorter period of time. So I deserved to gloat a bit after all the mud that had been slung at me by Burton Cummings in the media after I left the Guess Who. It was kind of a tongue-in-cheek poke at the Guess Who.

### "LOOKING OUT FOR #1"

What do you do with a bunch of jazz chords from your mentor, Lenny Breau? You write a song with them. Like "Blue Collar" a few years earlier, "Looking Out for #1" was another change of pace from BTO on our fifth album, 1975's *Head On*. It was also a chance for me to stretch out a bit on guitar. It's still among my most requested live songs and made the transition to my jazz career.

The chord progression I used on "Looking Out for #1" came from the *Mickey Baker Guitar Book* that Lenny Breau had told me about when I was a teenager. All the jazz stuff I played in my career to that point, including "Undun" and "Looking Out for #1," was either from Lenny or that Mickey Baker book. I was thrilled to play that song for Lenny much later. My verses on that song are the endings to just about every third jazz song. They're known as turn-around chord patterns because you reach the end of a verse and you turn around and start again. My chorus tag is from Ray Charles's "This Little Girl of Mine," which the Everly Brothers had also recorded. When I told Lenny I had taken all these jazz turn-around chord patterns he'd taught me and put them into a song, he gave me this inquisitive look.

"How can you make a song that starts with an ending? Won't people think the song is over?" That was Lenny. The song was "Looking Out for #1."

I didn't put a lot of deep thought into the lyrics. So many people have attached it to me and my own career, but I was just looking for something to sing over these chords and someone had mentioned something to me about sticking to your goals and following your dreams. I felt a little awkward at the end saying "I mean me," but you can't look after others if you don't take care of yourself. The song has become associated with me, but not intentionally on my part. The funny thing is that when Mercury Records put out a *BTO Greatest Hits* CD, "Looking Out for #1" was the first track on it. People buy it expecting to hear all this hard rock and instead they get this jazzy number.

### THE THUNDERBIRD TRAX

Burton Cummings and I got back together in 1987 to see if we could still collaborate. The tracks we recorded were very much of their time and sound pretty good years later.

In the late 80s Burton Cummings and I had been invited to the BMI awards in New York. We walk in and there's Yoko Ono accepting John Lennon's awards, and Leiber and Stoller—the great songwriting duo for Elvis, the Coasters, and the Drifters—receiving awards. The room was full of all these great writers, and Burton and I looked at each other as if to say, "Do we belong here?!" Then we were up onstage and all these great songwriters we revered are giving us a standing ovation for "These Eyes," our first big song. Afterwards everyone kept telling us, "Why don't you guys get back together and try it again?" I'd been out with BTO touring with Van Halen for ten and a half months. Now, when you play every night and you're doing sound checks and jamming with Eddie Van Halen, you really keep your chops up. I was playing really hot guitar at that point. So Burton and I decided to see if we still had the magic.

We got together at his place in L.A. and wrote a couple of songs, and then he came up to my place in White Rock, B.C., to write some more. He drove up from L.A. in this 1965 black Thunderbird. He pulled into my driveway in that cool car and I just went "Wow! Cool!" We spent our days in my front-yard tool shed—I'd had it converted in order to get away from my kids and write and record—working on songs and recording demos of them. We recorded ten songs. I played all the guitars, Burton did all the keyboards, and either I added bass or Burton played keyboard bass. We used a drum machine.

We sent out tapes of these songs to all the major labels, people like Clive Davis, Mo Ostin, and all the big shots. The response was generally "We love you guys and we love your stuff but who's gonna play it?" This was in the days before CDs and classic rock radio and all that. Everybody was saying, "Nobody wants all these classic rock dinosaurs." So we didn't get a record deal.

I moved a few times after that and the masters of those tracks somehow got lost in the shuffle. I'd given Burton a copy on cassette, and he'd thrown it in the trunk of his T-bird and driven back down to L.A. A few years later Burton called me and said he was moving a lot of his stuff back to Winnipeg. He'd bought a house in the city's classiest neighbourhood, Tuxedo. Then he said, "I'm selling one of my Thunderbirds. Do you want the black one?" Of course I said yes. When it arrived at my house I figured that instead of just driving it I should get it restored. So I called the Thunderbird Club in Vancouver and spoke to this wonderful guy named Bert who restored it for me. While he was doing the restoration, he handed me a box of stuff that he'd found in the car—stuff that falls out or is thrown in the back seat—and in the box among the pencils, tire gauge, manual, and candy wrappers was a little tape. I had mixed the songs on a Hi 8 movie-camera tape because at the time that was the only thing that was digital. I called my bass player, Richard Cochrane, who'd since bought my Hi 8 tape player from me, but he'd sold it to another guy who in turn had sold it. But finally we traced it back. When I got hold of it I put this little tape on, and it was the lost masters for those Bachman-Cummings sessions in my tool shed. For our 2006 Bachman-Cummings tour we released these tracks and called the CD *The Thunderbird Trax*. We quickly got some photos taken of the T-bird for the cover, Burton and I both wrote some liner notes, and we released it ourselves, no record label. We sold it at our concerts with the merchandise and it sold out almost immediately.

## *My Picks*

"AMERICAN DREAM" by Bachman-Cummings
(on *The Thunderbird Trax*)

"BLUE COLLAR" by BTO

"GIMME YOUR MONEY PLEASE" by BTO

"HEY YOU" by BTO

"LET IT RIDE" by BTO

"LOOKING OUT FOR #1" by BTO

"TAKIN' CARE OF BUSINESS" by BTO

"YOU AIN'T SEEN NOTHING YET" by BTO

# Close Encounters of the Six-String Kind, Part 2

## FESTIVAL EXPRESS

I was back home in Winnipeg in the summer of 1970 after leaving the Guess Who when the Festival Express came to town. It was a tour of the hottest acts in rock music at the time, who were travelling across Canada on a specially equipped Canadian National Railway chartered train. The lineup included the Band, Janis Joplin, the Grateful Dead, Mountain, Ian and Sylvia, Delaney and Bonnie and Friends, and Eric Andersen, among others. The whole thing was organized by promoter Ken Walker and backed by Thor Eaton of the Eaton's department store dynasty. The train stopped in Winnipeg for a concert on Canada Day, July 1, 1970. I wasn't booked or anything, but I played Festival Express in Winnipeg. I just walked onstage between acts while they were setting up equipment and did a brief acoustic interlude. No one really announced me. I just came out assuming people in Winnipeg would know who I was. Unfortunately, I don't think they did for the first few minutes. Then someone shouted out, "Hey, it's Randy Bachman."

I was so nervous that I ended up spelling "American woman" wrong. I was doing the "I say A, M, E ..." and I missed a letter. I was going to do a whole mini set, but I got so flustered by that flub that I walked off halfway through. I was just out of my element. I wasn't a solo acoustic performer and I didn't have a band. It was embarrassing. But I'm not sure anyone really knew who I was, so when I left I don't think anyone noticed or cared. I came back out later and joined Delaney and Bonnie onstage along with Leslie West for their big jam at the end of their set.

I also jammed on the train in this elegant parlour car. I was sitting there with Jerry Garcia and other members of the Grateful Dead, Janis Joplin, Delaney and Bonnie and their band, guys from the Band, Leslie West from Mountain. Players would wander into the room, pull up a chair, plug into one of the little amps they had or sit at the drum kit in the corner, and just join in the flow of the ongoing jams. I played all this rambling blues rock music. The smoke was so thick I opened a window and sat beside it. Guys were passing joints around, but I'd just say "No thanks" and it would get passed to the next guy. As the drugs and booze circulated around the room the playing got slower, lazier, and sloppier. But I was so charged to be playing with these people that my adrenaline was pumping. I just wanted to play with anybody, and since I'd left the Guess Who I hadn't played with anyone. I overheard someone say, "Who's the guy by the window with all the energy?" I was pumped while they were stoned.

### THE BEE GEES

Way back in early '73, Bachman-Turner Overdrive (me, Fred Turner, and my brothers Tim and Robbie) was just starting to happen. Our first album was out but we didn't have any hits yet. So we were thrilled to be invited to play on *The Midnight Special*, a Friday late-night rock 'n' roll concert-type show. The Bee Gees were hosting that night. So we arrived with our gear for the load-in during the night only to have the guys from the show tell us, "Okay, you have to be back here by six-thirty in the morning."

"What? I thought this was a late-night show?!"

So they tell us, "Yeah, it is. All the kids come in around five-thirty in the evening and the stars come soon after. But all the lesser-known artists have to come in a lot earlier and tape their spots. Then they edit it into the show and make it look like it's live in front of the audience." A lot of people don't realize that sometimes what they're watching is fake. I've been on television shows where we've had to lip-synch our songs on contrived sets in front of a fake audience. I've learned to expect anything in the entertainment business.

Then they add, "Oh, and by the way, there won't be anybody else here, so just come in and mime to your songs and we'll tape them."

So we get to our hotel, catch maybe three or four hours sleep, and come back to the television studio for six-thirty in the morning to tape our songs.

As we arrive, to our surprise, the Bee Gees, the hosts that night, were there to meet us. We met them all and shook hands. Here we were, the Bachman brothers—Randy, Tim, and Robbie—meeting the Gibb brothers—Barry, Robin, and Maurice. So I asked them why they were here so early, and they told us that they thought our band was great and that we were also a brother band like them. We became good friends from that point on.

After Maurice died, the other two Gibb brothers kind of went into hibernation. But in recent years we started running into Robin Gibb in the U.K. He was coming out of his shell a lot more, and we'd see him at various songwriter events. At the twenty-fifth anniversary of *Saturday Night Fever* at the BBC, he came out and sang a few songs. And I recently heard that Robin and Barry were reuniting to do some live dates. If you get the chance, go see them. They're incredible. They're like the Beatles, having written hundreds of great songs.

## DICK CLARK'S ROCKIN' NEW YEAR'S EVE

Here's another example of the "magic" of television. BTO got the call to play *Dick Clark's Rockin' New Year's Eve* in 1976. It was with Dick Clark himself as host, and disco diva Donna Summer was one of the guests along with us. Now, they don't actually film these things on New Year's Eve. They film it in September in Los Angeles at the old Copacabana club. They get all the kids from UCLA and get them to dress up as if it's a New Year's Eve ball in their ball gowns and suits. It's like a movie set, and the whole thing is filmed like a movie. Meanwhile outside it's hot and sunny and still summer. I used to watch it every year before that and never knew. On the show with us was the Miami Sound Machine with Gloria Estefan singing, KC and the Sunshine Band, and Donna Summer.

## THE STRANGELOVES

Sometimes even the band itself can be a fake. I remember we played with this group called the Strangeloves once when we were touring the U.S. with the original Guess Who back in 1965. They were all hype. They claimed to be three brothers, Miles, Giles, and Niles Strange, who were sheep herders from the bushes of Australia and who played these big drums made of sheepskin. But they were just a bunch of guys from New York, songwriters/record producers Bob Feldman, Jerry Goldstein, and Richard Gottehrer, who used to be studio musicians. "I Want Candy," "Cara-Lin," and "Night Time" were great pop singles. The only problem was that there was no such band as the Strangeloves. These three guys had concocted the elaborate story about the band and put a hired group of musicians on the road as the Strangeloves. They would start by beating these giant drums on stage, then they'd play their hits. There's always an element of hype and myth in rock 'n' roll, and these guys were able to milk it for a while.

## TROOPER

BTO's manager, Bruce Allen, and his partner, Sam Feldman, had a pet band they'd been working with in the local clubs around Vancouver by the name of Applejack. The band had a lot going for them: singer Ra Maguire and guitarist Brian Smith did the writing, and they were a great team. Sam Feldman asked me if I'd like to check them out to see if I might be able to help them. By this time BTO were so huge that I'd been given my own vanity record label. Applejack had reached a level where their next step was to record.

They were playing the Royal Arms Hotel in New Westminster a couple of blocks from my house. It was an easy stroll from my place, so I went and met the guys and liked what I heard. They already had some original material. I suggested they drop the Applejack name because I remembered a British Merseybeat group of the same name. So they came up with Trooper.

We got Trooper signed to MCA Records, and by that time they were ready to go into the studio. We had run through their original numbers so often I knew them backwards and forwards. I took them down to Kaye-Smith Studios in Seattle, where I knew everybody from recording there with BTO. We banged out the tracks over a week only to discover that the tape operator—the person who rolls the tape machines while you record, making sure the sound is captured on tape—had altered the tape heads. They were not aligned properly, so the recordings were unusable. That meant a week's worth of work was unusable. I was under the gun for time because I was due on tour with BTO, so the manager at Kaye-Smith gave us free time to complete the album. I said to the guys in Trooper, "Remember how you used to run through all your tunes back to back for me in rehearsals? Well, guess what? We're doing them all again on Monday."

So on Monday we recorded all the songs again, the entire album. Tuesday we added overdubs and Wednesday I mixed the tracks. We had their debut album ready to go by the end of the week. The album took off when it was released.

Trooper were a huge success across Canada because their singles were radio friendly and their albums and live shows really rocked. I was determined that they not be just a BTO clone. I wanted to make sure their sound was different. I think one of the reasons Trooper sounded different from BTO was the absence of a rhythm guitar. BTO always had a strong heavy rhythm sound that I took from early rock 'n' roll. I added chunky rhythm guitar to BTO tracks almost like the horn-section riffs in those old Fats Domino/Little Richard recordings. A song like "Gimme Your Money Please" simulates horn parts on the rhythm guitar using heavy-gauge strings. That was an essential ingredient in BTO that wasn't in Trooper. Trooper also had a more vocal sound than BTO.

Trooper represents Canadian 70s radio rock at its best and most rockin'. I admit I was a little bit prudish and didn't want them to record "Raise a Little Hell" on their first album. I actually tried to get them to change it to "Raise a Little Howl," but Ra and Brian stuck to their guns, and they were right. "Raise a Little Hell" is the ultimate Canadian party song.

I produced five albums with Trooper, but after that the band changed and announced that they were now ready to produce themselves. It was an amicable parting. I still see Ra from time to time and we talk fondly about those days.

### LITTLE RICHARD

We had recorded the *Head On* album and I was in L.A. mixing it when I realized that a couple of tracks could use some boogie woogie–type piano on them. So I told our manager, Bruce Allen, to see if he could get Elton John. Turned out Elton was unavailable.

"I need someone who can play rock 'n' roll piano like Little Richard," I told Bruce.

"Why don't you ask Little Richard?" was his reply. "He

just played a club here in Vancouver. His brother Payton is his manager. I'll give him a call."

Playing with Little Richard was like a dream come true. He was one of my first rock 'n' roll heroes. A couple of hours later Bruce called me back.

"Little Richard thinks BTO are great. He'll play on your album."

So we set up the session for Monday at noon. I wanted Richard to play on two songs, "Take It Like a Man" and "Stay Alive." The day before the session, Payton called me and asked what key the songs were in. So I told him they were both in the key of A. I could sense from him that there might be a problem. Then he said, "Can you change them to another key?" I told him the tracks were already recorded and all I was doing was adding Richard's piano as an overdub.

The next day it's two-thirty before Richard finally shows up. I'm sitting in the studio killing time playing guitar, so as Richard walks through the door, I started playing "Lucille."

There he was, every inch Mr. Rock 'n' Roll, decked out in a white ermine coat over a cape and an orange jumpsuit with a silver R on it and carrying a travelling makeup case. He had on the eyeliner and mascara.

I played the tape of the first song for him in the control booth and told him the chord changes. It was a simple number. "What key's it in?" asked Richard. "A." "Are you sure?"

"Yes. It's just A, D, A, E, and an F#m."

As he's looking at me, Richard spaces out when I say F#m as if I'm speaking in another language. I had him try playing to the tape, but he couldn't do it. He couldn't follow a simple chord chart. Payton called me aside and said, "Richard's really embarrassed." So I tried one more thing. I went into the studio with my guitar, plugged into a little Fender amp, and sat beside him at the piano.

"Let's warm up a bit and just jam."

So I played some of his songs and he starts wailing away. They're all in G, C, or D. But the minute I said A or F#m, he was lost. I told my engineer, Mark Smith, to vary the speed of the tape, which slows it down and alters the pitch. Mark took a tuner and got the speed of the song a tone lower to G. "When I give you the signal, start rolling the tape," I told him.

With Richard thinking he's only playing along with me on guitar, we tried "Take It Like a Man," but now it's in G. I gave Mark the signal to roll tape and Richard takes off, totally rockin', pounding out 16th notes, 32nd notes, and 64th notes as I yell, "Play it, Richard!" You can actually hear that on the track. Afterwards Mark gives me the okay sign. He got it all on tape. So I said, "Richard, come into the control room and listen."

"What are you talkin' about?"

Mark brought the song back up to normal speed and now Richard's looking at Payton.

"Who's that playing piano?"

"You are!"

"Really?! What key's it in?"

"A," I tell him and he looks stunned.

"Hallelujah! Praise the Lord! I can play in A!" And he dropped to his knees.

We did the same thing with "Stay Alive," and Richard nailed it on the slower speed. Here he was, one of the original rockers, and he only knew a few chords. He was the master of three-chord rock 'n' roll. The poor guy never knew about variable speed on tapes. When Little Richard came through Vancouver again a few months later, we all went to see him and presented him with a crown as the king of rock 'n' roll.

### JOHNNY PAYCHECK

BTO often played down in the southern U.S. at festivals alongside country music acts. There wasn't much of a distinction between rock and the kind of rugged outlaw country music at these festivals in the mid 70s. We had a promoter out of Nashville who booked us on several of these kinds of shows. He'd pair us up with country acts and it was cool. We played with Hank Williams Jr., Sawyer Brown, the Allman Brothers, Willie Nelson, Wet Willie.

We were booked at this one festival where Johnny Paycheck was also on the bill. I wanted to meet him and say hello for my friend Charlie Fach, head of Mercury Records, our label. Charlie told me I had to go meet Johnny because he's a cool guy. "Take This Job and Shove It" became a working man's anthem in the latter 70s and made Johnny Paycheck a star after years of paying his dues on the roadhouse circuit. Johnny joined the "Outlaw Country" movement that included Willie Nelson, Waylon Jennings, and Kris Kristofferson. So I figured I'd go introduce myself. I headed over to where all the tour buses were parked for all the acts and spotted Johnny Paycheck's bus. As I rounded the corner towards his bus, I heard this high-pitched growl and I stopped in my tracks. There, chained to the front of Johnny's bus, was an ocelot. Apparently his tour bus had been robbed not long before that, and while everyone else hired personal security or bought guard dogs to bring along on the road to protect their belongings while they were onstage performing, Johnny had bought an ocelot. They're like leopards. These are the most beautiful animals, sleek and gorgeous. But it growled again at me, so I left Johnny and his bus and his ocelot alone. I never did meet Johnny Paycheck.

### CAT STEVENS

I first met Cat Stevens (born Steven Demetre Giorgiou) in England when we went there in early 1967. He was just a brand-new songwriter and scored a hit record by the Tremeloes with "Here Comes My Baby" not long after that. I didn't see him for about ten years. I was in L.A. recording a solo album, *Survivor,* and staying at a place in Beverley Hills called L'Hermitage. I used to go up to the pool on the top of the hotel, and I'd see Cat Stevens there and we'd talk about music and songwriting. He seemed like a normal guy.

A few weeks later, as I was finishing up the recording for the album, I was getting into the elevator at the hotel when the doors open and it's Cat Stevens. He's standing there and he had totally changed. He had cut his hair and was wearing robes. Apparently he'd been out surfing in Malibu, got caught in the riptide, and was dragged under. It's happened to me and it's a very scary sensation, as if you're being held under water by some unseen demons. Cat thought he was drowning, and while this was happening to him he made a promise to God that if he would help him out of this, save his life, he would dedicate the rest of his life to God. He was washed up on the beach, and true to his word, he devoted his life to serving God.

### LAWRENCE WELK

Me and Lawrence Welk? Go figure.

Lawrence Welk, the schmaltz band leader with the bubble machine, owned a record label called Vanguard Records, and they had a publishing company. In the 70s I was invited to meet with their publishing company in L.A. because I had some songs and they wanted to hear them. So I go to their offices, a big multistorey office building in downtown Santa Monica right near the ocean. I'm there at Lawrence Welk's office on the twelfth floor or so. He owns the whole building. I look outside the window and there's a balcony that goes all around the building. The Welk building occupies the entire city block. The balcony is enclosed in Plexiglas and the floor is covered in Astroturf, and on the Astroturf are little flags. Lawrence Welk had the whole balcony set out as a four-hole golf course so that he could go out there and play some golf, hitting the ball around the building. I'd never seen anything like it. We didn't do a deal, but I was impressed with his building.

### THE POINTER SISTERS

In the late 70s I was in L.A. recording my solo album, *Survivor.* Burton Cummings was recording a solo album at the same time and I was doing some recording with him. In the studio we were using the same backing guys, who later became Toto. They had started out as Boz Scaggs's recording and backing band and were on his big hit "Lowdown." So they were hanging out at Richard Perry's recording studio, Studio 55, on Melrose Avenue. Richard was producing Burton's album as well as people like Eric Carmen, Ringo Starr, Cher, and the Pointer Sisters. I was recording either with Burton or on my album during the week.

On this particular weekend my kids had come down to join me. We were staying at a hotel right downtown in Hollywood and were going to go to Disneyland on Saturday for the day. So we all get up that morning and I foolishly take them to a place called Carl's Jr. for breakfast. I wouldn't recommend Carl's Jr. for breakfast. It's a fast-food burger place. After we eat, we're in the car heading down Melrose to the freeway to get to Anaheim. From Hollywood to Anaheim is about a two-hour drive. Not long after we're in the car, one of my daughters, who was three at the time, gets sick and throws up all over herself. I'm thinking, I can't make her stay in these clothes all day at Disneyland; she needs to be cleaned up. We were on Melrose and I knew the security code to get into Studio 55, so I parked in front, punched the code, and went in.

The Pointer Sisters—Anita, June, and Ruth Pointer—were recording at the time. They'd started out singing backup for many recording artists before launching their own successful recording career in the mid 70s. By the time I met them, they were already huge stars. They had sung on a track for Burton and on one of mine, so they knew me and saw me coming in with this little three-year-old. They said hello and asked me why I was there. I told them I'd dropped in to clean up my daughter who'd had an accident.

"Let us do that. You're a guy. We'll take care of her." So they took her by the hand to the bathroom, stood her up in the sink, and rinsed her and her clothes off. They were all mothers themselves and knew how to take care of a little kid. It was all just a normal thing, no star trips or anything like that. That's my memory of the Pointer Sisters. Wonderful ladies.

### THE BEACH BOYS

I could relate to the Beach Boys and Brian Wilson being in a band with his brothers because often in my career I had one or two of my brothers in a band with me. I became a big fan of the Beach Boys early on. Originally from Hawthorne, California, the Wilson brothers—Brian, Dennis, and Carl—plus cousin Mike Love and friend Al Jardine are an American institution. They were like the alternative Beatles, the American Beatles. In the 60s they captured teenage America's fascination with surfing, cars, and girls. So imagine my thrill when years later I got to write songs with Carl Wilson of the Beach Boys!

After I left BTO I had a band in the late 70s called Iron Horse. Carl Wilson heard our album and invited us to open for the Beach Boys on their tour. What was special about this tour was that Brian Wilson had just come out of therapy and was on the road with the band again, accompanied by his personal therapist, Eugene Landy. Most people know about Brian Wilson's problems over the years.

When we'd played Beach Boys songs in the Guess Who, I'd sung the high parts. I loved doing that. So every night after Iron Horse's set I would change my clothes and sit in the wings and sing along with them. I'd sing all my old parts in "I Get Around" and "California Girls." But the real kicker for me was being invited by Carl Wilson to the Caribou Ranch in Colorado to write songs with him for the next Beach Boys album. For a kid from Winnipeg this was a dream come true. Carl was such an easygoing guy and great to write with because we both respected each other as artists. He and I wrote a song called "Keep the Summer Alive," and it became the title song of their next album. Now how cool was that? Fred Turner and I later had a band called Union and we recorded "Keep the Summer Alive" on our one and only album, *On Strike*.

### MASON WILLIAMS AND "CLASSICAL GAS"

Back in the 60s when you picked up a guitar, you would play "Classical Gas." That song was written by Mason Williams, who was a comedy writer on *The Smothers Brothers Comedy Hour*. One day he got tired of trying to come up with funny gags or setup and payoff lines. When you write for a comedy show every line has to be funny, and that's not always easy to do. So instead he picked up his guitar and wrote something he called "Classical Gasoline." He played it for the producers of the show, and they liked it and decided to put a collage of images and visuals around it. This was the 60s, and *Laugh-In* was on TV with all these psychedelic images—amoebas, paramecia, and other weird things throbbing and moving across the screen—which was all part of the psychedelic movement at the time. So they put "Classical Gasoline" on *The Smothers Brothers* show basically as a backup or soundtrack to this psychedelic collage of visuals. But what happened afterwards was that people started requesting the song or asking where they could buy the record. So it was released as a 45 and ultimately went on to sell millions of records.

A little while later Mason Williams came up to Canada to do a CBC television show taped in Toronto called *Guitar*. He wanted to have a number of guitar players on the show. He had himself, of course, and he had the great Canadian jazz guitarist Ed Bickert, who was born in Manitoba, and country picker extraordinaire Merle Travis. They were going to have the great Les Paul on the show, but Les Paul suffers from vertigo and couldn't travel. When you have vertigo the whole world spins around and you can't stand up. They have to strap you to a bed until you recover from a spell of it. So I got the call to be on the show.

I flew in and met Mason Williams, and he taught me "Classical Gas," which was very cool. He wrote it all out for me by hand and signed it; I still have it. And I can still play it, too. Anyway, it was pretty cold in Toronto at the time and Merle Travis stayed warm by drinking. He was pretty much inebriated the whole time we were in Toronto. When it came time to record the show, we were all playing alternate four- or eight-bar sections of "Classical Gas." But when it came time for Merle's section, he blew it. He was so overcome with "feeling so good" that he flubbed his part. So the producer stopped the show and started it again. This was all in front of a live audience, but this kind of thing can often happen and you just stop tape and start it over again. Someone breaks a string or something. Audiences are used to this.

We started the song again and I could see that Merle was playing behind the beat. He was just not making it. So when it gets to his part and the camera is on his fingers, I could tell he wasn't going to be able to play it, so I played it off camera for him. I can play that finger-picking style of his. I learned it as a kid from watching Lenny Breau. So they pulled back on the camera for a shot of Merle with everybody else as if nothing had happened. For all intents and purposes it looked like he was playing the licks. After the show he came up to me and said, "Thank you for doing that for me. You're my little buddy. You saved me because I wouldn't have been able to do it." No one watching the show ever knew.

Afterwards, Merle said he had a gift for me. He then gave me his spare Gibson Super 400 model guitar with his name in pearl lettering on the fretboard. It looked brand new even though it was decades old. I told him I couldn't take it, but he insisted. So I took it back to my room at the Four Seasons hotel across from the CBC studios. The next morning Merle's wife knocked on my door and asked for the guitar back. "He's always giving that thing away," she told me. I was happy to give it back, and it's now in the Country Music Hall of Fame in Nashville. But I have a great photograph with Merle and me that he signed, "To my little buddy, Randy. God bless, Merle."

### HENRY MANCINI

If Henry Mancini had written only "Moon River" he'd still be one of the greatest songwriters of the twentieth century. "The Days of Wine and Roses," "Peter Gunn Theme," "The Pink Panther," "Charade," plus dozens of movie scores including *Breakfast at Tiffany's, The Great Race, Hatari!, The Thorn Birds, Darling Lili,* and *Victor Victoria* earned Henry some twenty Grammys and four Oscars.

In the 80s I had a song-publishing deal with Arista. Clive Davis had left CBS Records and started Arista Records and Music. So Clive said to me, "Why don't you come out to L.A. and meet our team?" I flew out there and met Billy Michelle, who was the head guy at Arista music publishing at the time. Billy introduced me to his assistant. All I caught was "This is Chris M something." I didn't hear the last name. Chris was a real nice guy and showed me around the office. Then he asked me if I wanted to come over to his house for dinner. "Sure," I said.

As I'm driving up to his house, I notice a name on the mailbox: Mancini. I'm wondering if it's just a coincidence. I get to the door, Chris answers, and he invites me in and says, "This is my dad." And standing there is Henry Mancini. Chris Mancini was the son of renowned composer Henry Mancini. I was stunned. How many guitar players picked up a guitar when they were just starting out and played the "Peter Gunn" riff?

Throughout the evening I'm flashing back in my head on all the great songs Henry Mancini has written: the theme from *The Pink Panther,* "Baby Elephant Walk," "Moon River," and on and on. One of the greatest composers of all time and I'm having dinner with him. After dinner Henry sat down at the piano. Clearly he was composing or working on ideas, so I wasn't going to go up to him and say, "Duh, can you play 'Moon River'?"

## SAMMY HAGAR AND EDDIE VAN HALEN

While we were getting BTO off the ground again in the mid 80s, working constantly out on the road, my old friend Sammy Hagar called me out of the blue.

"I've just joined Van Halen," he announced over the phone. "We're going out on the road and we really need a strong opening act. Will you open for us?"

"For how long?"

"Let's road-test it for a week and see how it works out."

This was a terrific opportunity for us to get some high-profile exposure. Van Halen touring with a new lead singer would be big news.

Sammy was a long-time BTO fan and had previously been writing songs with me at my home just across the border in Lynden, Washington. In 1986 he replaced David Lee Roth in Van Halen and they needed a kick-ass opening act on their first tour with Sammy as lead singer. So he said to me on the phone, "BTO just popped out of nowhere. We all love BTO. Every song the fans will love."

We'd been slugging it out on the road, travelling on the cheap for two years, when Fred needed to be at home with his wife and teenage sons. So we'd agreed to take some time off, and it was during that time that Sammy called me. It was a Friday and he needed an answer by Monday morning. The four members of Van Halen had unanimously agreed to BTO as their choice for opening act.

Sammy said, "We need an opening act that will be so powerful that no one will be screaming, 'Where's David?' You guys will get them rocking doing all your hits, bam bam bam, we'll do a quick turnover and come out swinging and hit 'em hard so that no one will even remember David Lee Roth. But we've gotta have an answer by Monday."

After I hung up the phone I immediately called Fred, but there was no answer. I kept calling every hour, but nothing. Then one of his kids answered and told me that Fred and his wife had gone on a short vacation and wouldn't be back until Monday or Tuesday.

Monday morning arrived and I had to call Sammy back. My son, Tal, was a teenager then and a huge Van Halen fan. Eddie Van Halen was his idol. So he was over the moon that his dad might be touring with his heroes. As much as anything I wanted to do it to impress Tally that his dad was cool. At this point it was only for a week, nothing more, so I called Sammy that Monday.

"Some of us are in, some of us aren't," I told him.

"What do you mean?"

"I can't get hold of Fred Turner."

"Who have you got?"

"Me, my brother Tim who can play bass, and Garry Peterson on drums. But basically our lead singer is gone."

"Who sings 'Takin' Care of Business'?" Sammy asked.

"I do."

"Who sings 'You Ain't Seen Nothing Yet'?"

"That's me as well."

"Who sings 'Hey You'?"

"Me again."

"And who sings 'Let It Ride'?"

"That's Fred."

"Okay, we'll take you. Van Halen is coming without its old lead singer so you guys can come without your lead singer. Let's give it a shot."

We went on to do the entire 5150 tour, over a hundred dates opening for Van Halen, and we had a ball the whole time. We travelled in a station wagon while they travelled in their luxury tour bus. And every night we rocked the biggest arenas across the States.

During that same 5150 tour, I was really surprised one night as I warmed up in the dressing room playing my Lenny Breau/ Chet Atkins stuff when Eddie Van Halen popped his head in and asked, "How do you do that?" I would ask him how he did all his guitar tricks, too.

One night we were in Knoxville, Tennessee. My phone rang at three in the morning. I'm in bed sleeping. I pick it up and the voice says, "Randolph?" Nobody calls me Randolph except my mother when she was angry with me.

I said, "Yes?"

"It's Edward." Nobody called Eddie Van Halen "Edward."

He tells me he wants me to come to his suite and gives me the number. We're in the same hotel, but he's got a suite. I'm in a room. This is Eddie Van Halen, one of the greatest guitar players in the world, so how do you say no? I went to his suite, and as I'm getting out of the elevator, I can see him sitting on the floor outside his door. He's got an acoustic guitar with him and he's playing. He tells me to pull up a rug, so I sit down and Eddie says, "I just heard that my best friend from school days died. Suicide. I can't be there for him and his family because we're on tour, but I'll get back for his memorial service. These are my thoughts about him for tonight. Will you just sit here while I play this for him? I really feel his spirit here with me tonight."

"Sure." So I sat there while he played for two and a half hours. Eddie Van Halen played his heart out. He did things I'd never heard anyone play before. I wish I'd had a tape recorder with me that night.

### RINGO STARR

I was such a huge Beatles fan that when *A Hard Day's Night* opened at the Garrick Theatre in downtown Winnipeg in the summer of 1964, I was there the moment the doors opened and I stayed in that theatre all day. I must have seen it ten times or more. I loved that movie.

Jump ahead some thirty years. It's 1995 and the phone rings at my house in White Rock. Ironically, the night before I'd been watching *The Making of A Hard Day's Night* on PBS. I pick up the phone and on the other end is this voice that sounds familiar. He says, "Hello, Randy. I'd like you to be in my band."

So I'm thinking, "Who is this?"

When he said "This is Ringo Starr," my reaction was like those old Jackie Gleason *Honeymooners* moments where he would go, "a hummina hummina ..."

He told me who was going to be in the band with him: his son Zach on drums, Billy Preston and the Rascals' Felix Cavaliere on keyboards, Mark Farner from Grand Funk Railroad on guitar, and the Who's John Entwistle on bass. Wow! What a great lineup.

After I hung up the phone I shouted out to my wife, Denise, "Guess who just called me!" I phoned up all my friends and said, "You won't believe who I just talked to!" I was like that same kid at the Garrick Theatre back in Winnipeg.

We ended up having rehearsals in Vancouver, which was perfect for me. We toured all over America and went to Japan, and it was all fabulous. I was totally gaga the whole tour. Ringo knew I was a real fan, not merely one of the musicians in the band. I'd look over my shoulder during "Takin' Care of Business" and grin from ear to ear because there was Ringo Starr backing me up on my own song. He was so much fun to be around. Me being a Beatlemaniac and an avid collector, I brought a stack of things to the first rehearsal for Ringo to sign—albums, singles, books. As he walked in he looked at the pile and simply said, "Pick two." He just couldn't sign everything for everyone or he'd have been there all day.

Once the tour started, we could see how he was just a normal guy like us. Everyone called him Richie. No star trips and everyone treated equally. When he travelled first class, we all travelled first class. If he had a private plane, we all took it. If it was on a bus sweating with no air conditioning, he was there with everyone. He was so humble and down to earth.

We celebrated Ringo's birthday when we were playing in Chicago, and for the occasion we rented a big restaurant for a party. Beforehand I had called Denise at home. "What do I give a guy who has everything?" She came up with a novel idea.

"Why don't you buy Ringo his own star?"

Some astronomers in an observatory near Chicago had discovered a cluster of new stars in the galaxy, and you could name one of them for a nominal fee. Denise took care of the details and a certificate arrived at the hotel from this famous observatory, along with a star chart identifying and circling the star you'd named. The certificate proclaimed that from henceforth this star would be known as Ringo Star. What a great present! Ringo was knocked out. This is what you get a guy who has everything—you get him his own celestial body.

### JOHN ENTWISTLE

For the Ringo Starr tour we were all told to bring a small amp: fifty watts, maybe a hundred at best, and you could take a tube out or keep the volume down. Everything is miked through the PA and is loud out in front of the stage, but we don't want a huge din of noise onstage. Felix Cavaliere showed up with a Hammond organ and a Leslie speaker cabinet, which isn't that powerful. Billy Preston had an electric piano and a small amp. Mark Farner and I had small amps.

Then John Entwistle arrives. With him he's brought a three thousand-watt stereo amplifier with two speaker cabinets the size of giant refrigerators that he places on either side of the drummers. Turns out he's actually pretty much deaf from all his years in the Who, and to him he's not loud. Except that Mark Farner and I can't hear our guitars over his thundering bass, and so we turn up to be heard over all this booming bass. This causes everyone to turn up. Ringo's out front trying to sing "With a Little Help from My Friends" and all of a sudden he can't hear himself singing. He keeps turning back and telling us all to turn down. John Entwistle just wouldn't turn down. He played an active bass, and I don't like those because they boost the sound of the bass too much.

He had a nine-volt battery powering active pickups, one pickup for each string! He would touch a string as you would tickle your own finger or flick a hair off your sweater, just barely caressing the strings, and it would go *BOOOOOOM Budda BOOOOOM Budda BOOOOOM!* Thunderous. He was a wonderful guy, very nice, polite and gracious, a true British gentleman. But he played excruciatingly loud, and there was no way we could get him to turn down.

Mark Farner and I lost our hearing on that tour. We had tinnitus, or ringing in the ears, afterwards. While playing with John Entwistle, we discovered that because his hearing was so shot after decades playing in the loudest band in the world, he needed to feel the pressure of the bass sound coming from his speakers. He had to have the rush of air from these incredibly loud speakers hitting him in the back in order to play.

## RINGO'S WIFE'S BIRTHDAY PARTY

A year after the tour, my wife Denise and I were invited to Ringo Starr's wife Barbara Bach's fortieth birthday party in Beverley Hills. She was an actress, and the two of them had met on the set of the movie *Caveman* and married in 1981. It was fabulous. The long, long driveway to the house was covered in a long red silk canopy, and at every turn there were tables with chocolates and sometimes a magician. The pool was covered over with Plexiglas with coloured lights under it, and that served as the dance floor. A big stage had been set up nearby with various instruments and amplifiers, and as the party wore on people would get up and do their songs.

At one point I got up on stage with the great bass player and producer Don Was as well as Brian Wilson, Stevie Nicks, Tom Petty, and Hank Ballard. Hank's the guy who wrote and first recorded "The Twist." Chubby Checker covered it and made it a hit. So here we all are doing the Twist on the Plexiglas pool in Beverley Hills. Can you imagine that, me, a kid from the North End of Winnipeg? It was the most amazing party I'd ever been to.

## B.B. KING

Back in the early Guess Who days, we played a college bookers' showcase in Memphis, Tennessee. This is where all the state-college bookers in the region come to check out bands or performers, and if they like you they block-book you for a month or so in all the colleges nearby. You get fifteen minutes to go out there and do your best stuff, all your tricks, to impress these bookers, who are mostly college kids.

We were on this showcase sandwiched between Roy Clark and the great blues guitarist B.B. King. Roy Clark is a great guitar player, even though he does all these goofy things and plays up the country hick image. We followed him and did our little shtick as the Guess Who. We all shared a dressing room, which was simply a classroom where you laid your coats and stuff on the desks. So everyone is in this same classroom-cum-dressing room. After our set B.B. King comes up to me and says, "You're a really great guitar player, but you make it look too easy."

And I said, "What do you mean?"

So he told me I should be making a face or grimacing when I hit the big notes. "You need to wince like you're feeling that note in your soul, the pain and the anguish in that note." He scrunched his eyes up and played a note to show me what he meant.

I can play a solo with a dead straight expression or a smile on my face, but ever since then I make that "guitar" face. It's kind of like acting, but you're putting more into that note and audiences can feel it, too. Your whole body is into it, not just your fingers. Eric Clapton does the same thing.

After my time with Ringo Starr's All-Starrs, Ringo went back to England. NorthWest Airlines was opening up a bunch of new routes, including more Canadian ones. So the airline hired the All-Starr band to play all these parties and gigs, letting people know that NorthWest had these new destinations. We became the NorthWest All-Stars. Our final gig was at Cobo Hall in Detroit opening for B.B. King.

We go out and do our set. Mark Farner does his Grand Funk songs, Felix Cavaliere does his Young Rascals hits, John Entwistle does "Boris the Spider" from the Who, Billy Preston does his thing, and I do my BTO hits. After our set, B.B. King comes on, but before he starts to play he tells us not to leave. Meanwhile all our gear is being packed up because we're shipping our stuff back to our homes since the tour is done.

B.B. King is doing his set and then, I think it was during his big number "The Thrill Is Gone," he starts inviting us out one at a time. Mark Farner comes out first and picks up B.B.'s spare guitar onstage and starts to play. As each guy is called out to join B.B. in the song, his band members hand over their instruments or vacate their keyboards. I'm the last guy he calls and as I come out there's no guitar. Mine are already packed away. So as I walk out one of B.B.'s two drummers stands up and hands me his sticks. I lean over to him and say, "I'm a guitar player!"

He replies, "That's okay. Just fake it."

Now, I can't play drums to save my life. Anyone who's ever played with me knows what a train wreck that is. So here I am sitting at the drums attempting to keep it together, all the while trying to look cool, when B.B. turns to me and yells, "Take it!"

"What?!"

So I start flailing away, smashing and crashing around like Keith Moon on acid. It was awful but it was hilarious. That was my big B.B. King onstage moment.

### BO DIDDLEY

It's the summer of 1969 and the Guess Who are asked to appear at the Seattle Pop Festival. Imagine these musicians all together: the Doors, the Byrds, Led Zeppelin, Ike and Tina Turner, Ten Years After, the Youngbloods, Charles Lloyd, the Flying Burrito Brothers, and Bo Diddley. That was the first time I saw Bo Diddley perform. The Bo Diddley beat, that "shave and a haircut, two bits" hambone rhythm, was an important part of the early evolution of rock 'n' roll. Just check out Buddy Holly, the Animals, or the Rolling Stones. His hits—"Hey Bo Diddley," "I'm a Man," "Road Runner," and "Who Do You Love"—revolutionized rock 'n' roll rhythm.

Many, many years later I was invited to the Georgia Music Hall of Fame in Macon, about ninety minutes south of Atlanta. They were hosting a show on Gretsch guitars because they have a large Gretsch display in the museum. The closing act was Bo Diddley. I had this handbill from the Seattle Pop Festival some forty years earlier that listed all the acts on the festival. They didn't have posters, only handbills, and I'd kept one. So I had a copy made and I'd brought it with me to show Bo Diddley that evening. When I met him I gave it to him, and he was so excited. He said, "My grandkids didn't believe I played with Led Zeppelin and the Doors, so now I can show them it's true! This is fantastic."

After I did my set, I left my guitar in the stand and took a seat in the audience. Then Bo came out with his band, some really heavy-duty players like Chuck Leavell from the Allman Brothers and Vinnie Colaiuta from Sting's band. Bo looks at my guitar on the stand and the empty seat beside it and asks, "Whose seat is that? Who's supposed to be here?"

"Me!" I replied from the audience.

"Well then, get on up here."

So I ended up playing his entire set with him. What a thrill for me.

### GEORGE MICHAEL

I knew of controversial British singer/songwriter George Michael from Wham back in the 1980s, but I'd never met him. I thought "Wake Me Up Before You Go-Go" was a real fun song. Then one evening when we were still living in White Rock, south of Vancouver, my phone rang. I picked it up and the voice said in a very English accent, "Hello, this is George Michael," and I said, "Really?!"

He replied "Yes," then asked me if I had any Gretsch guitars.

Are you kidding? So I told him, "Yes, I have three hundred of them."

"Could you pick out four or five and bring them down to the Bayshore Inn? I'm staying here overnight and shooting a video tomorrow and I'd like to use one of your guitars in my video."

I was thrilled because Wham was a big band at the time and he was just launching his solo career with his album *Faith*. When it came time to film the video for the title song, George called me. Some of my daughters were teenagers at the time and were pretty excited that George Michael had called their house. So I took some Gretsches down and he picked one to play during the video. He seemed like a pretty nice guy, but I didn't want him to take that guitar out of my sight. I was hoping he'd say "Come to the video shoot," and he did. It was in a big old warehouse somewhere in Vancouver. I took some of my daughters with me and he was very cool with them. Callianne was maybe two at the time and I took a photo of George holding her. She looks like a little doll in his arms. So when he came through Vancouver later to do a concert, I called up and got tickets and took all my daughters to see him. He's just a really great guy.

## JOE PASS

I was at a NAMM show back in the early 90s and jazz guitarist Joe Pass was scheduled to play at one of the booths. The NAMM show is the National Association of Music Merchants trade show, and it's huge. Humongous. Every instrument company is represented there. Lots of these companies will hire great players to be at their booth to demonstrate their new instruments—guitar, bass, drums, keyboards. I'd been listening to Joe Pass since Lenny Breau turned me on to him back in the very early 60s, before I was in the Guess Who. Joe Pass was a legendary jazz guitarist and I loved his playing. He'd worked with everyone from Frank

Sinatra, Tony Bennett, Oscar Peterson, and Duke Ellington to Ella Fitzgerald and Count Basie.

I got to the arena where they held the NAMM show early and went to where Joe was going to be playing. There were other guitar players there waiting with me. Joe arrives and I'm taken aback by how cranky he is. As Yogi Bear would say, "Sheeesh, what a grouch!" He was kind of short-tempered, curt and ordering people around. I remember at the time thinking, "Whoa, he could be a lot nicer to people." But when he got up to play, the tenseness and the lines in his face melted away. He just transported himself, and everyone watching, myself included, to another place. It was magical. You forgot all about the grouchy guy.

I learned soon afterwards that Joe Pass had cancer and passed away not long after that show. I was humbled that I'd had that moment with him and felt bad about the way I'd judged him. You should never judge people in the moment because there may be other circumstances they're going through. I was touched by his playing and I miss him.

### RITA MACNEIL

I was touring with my own band doing my "Every Song Tells a Story" show in 2002 and we were playing out in Cape Breton Island. This is Rita MacNeil's backyard. She's from Big Pond, Nova Scotia, and is a true Canadian superstar. There was a hush in the crowd just before we started and word came around that Rita and her son were in the audience. She's like royalty in Cape Breton Island. So we did the show and I was really hoping I would meet Rita afterwards. She's a great songwriter and a great Canadian. After our shows, once we've quickly towelled off, my band and I come out and sign everything people bring for us to sign: old vinyl albums or 45s, eight-tracks, CDs, photos, and maybe some of the merchandise we're selling after the show. It's kind of like the Garth Brooks thing or what Nashville country stars do: They stay until everyone's got what they have signed or posed for a photo with us.

Just as we're sitting down to start signing and meeting the fans, one of my band guys comes up to me and whispers in my ear.

"They've cleaned out the dressing room!"

Now that can mean one of two things. Either the janitor has come by and swept up in the room or we've been robbed. Unfortunately, it was the latter. Some thieves had snuck backstage, and as we were starting our signing session they'd cleaned us out of our valuables—backpacks, wallets, watches, credit cards, iPods, cameras. I'd checked out of my hotel just before we headed to the gig and I had all my valuables in a plastic Delta Hotel laundry bag. I'd just thrown it all in the bag and checked out. So when we went back to the dressing room, all that was left was this Delta Hotel bag with my stuff. I had to leave the table to deal with the police, who'd been called by the promoter. They were able to catch the guys, but by the time I got back out front to the lineup I was told Rita had left. So I missed meeting Rita MacNeil.

I saw her at the Juno Awards one year and she did her song about going down into the mines, "Working Man," and brought out all these miners in their mining hats onstage to sing it with her. It was very reminiscent of the time I saw Paul McCartney do "Mull of Kintyre" and he brought out the bagpipers from the Black Watch. Rita brought them onstage in the dark, and when their lights came on it was a very moving moment for everyone in the audience. So Rita, if you read this, please come to my next show in Cape Breton because I would very much like to meet you.

### THE SIMPSONS

I came home from a tour in mid 1999 to find a fax waiting for me from Sony Music, who controlled my song publishing. They were asking if I knew anything about *The Simpsons* television show wanting to license "Takin' Care of Business" and "You Ain't Seen Nothing Yet." I faxed them back saying, "Great, let them use them." I just thought they were probably going to have them playing in the background in Moe's bar. The next day a script arrived for me from *The Simpsons*. More than the two songs, they actually wanted Fred and me to speak on the show.

So I read through the script and it was absolutely incredible. I called the producers to say I was in and they arranged to fly me down to tape my part. They treated me like I was Tom Cruise or something—a limo at the airport, a suite at the finest hotel. A very classy organization. They treated Fred Turner the same.

The director worked with me on how to deliver my lines. They record your vocal first, and as you do so they videotape you so that the animators can pick up on your body movements. You don't record your part with the cast because it's too distracting. I would have been totally gaga if the person standing beside me started talking in the voice of Homer Simpson. I later attended a table read with the entire cast and was dumbstruck. I couldn't have done it with them present.

The script required me to say "Hello, Springfield!" as if I was walking out onstage. So I said, "Hello, Springfield." The director came over to me and said, "Are you playing for an audience of one person? You're on stage, it's a concert."

I tried adding a bit more force. "Hello, Springfield!"

"Randy, there's twenty thousand people in the audience."

"HELLO, SPRINGFIELD!!"

"Perfect. Give me three more like that."

As the story line went, I come out and say "Hello, Springfield," and Homer says to Bart, "Watch these guys, they're BTO!" and Bart says, "BTO?" So Homer tells him, "Yeah, they're Canada's answer to ELP. We didn't have a lot of time in the 70s so we only used initials."

I did all my lines alone, and when I was done they gave me a big box of *Simpsons* merchandise for myself and my kids and sent me on my way.

The episode was titled *Saddle Sore Galactica* and aired February 6, 2000. In it, Homer Simpson's favourite band, BTO, are performing at the Springfield bandshell and Fred and I speak to Homer.

Just before Christmas that year I received a package by courier. It was a Christmas present from Homer Simpson with a card and a little shiny black shopping bag with a dog tag on the handle that read: "Merry Christmas, Randy Bachman, *The Simpsons* 1999." Inside was a Swiss Army stopwatch with *The Simpsons* on the face in a beautiful leather case with the words "Merry Christmas from the Simpsons."

### SMASHY AND NICEY

In the early 1990s the weekly British comedy show *Harry Enfield's Television Programme* featured a regular skit in which two over-the-hill deejays, Smashy and Nicey, play a newer record and then smash it, ending the skit by playing their favourite song, BTO's "You Ain't Seen Nothing Yet." The skit was extremely popular and Smashy and Nicey became a phenomenon. All this was unknown to me.

I hadn't realized how much of an icon that song had become in the U.K. until I was flying from Germany to England in the mid 90s. The British flight attendant knew I was in a band but had no idea who I was or what band I was from. So she asked who I was. When I said Randy Bachman, it didn't register with her.

"Bachman-Turner Overdrive?"

Nothing.

"What other bands have you been in?" she inquired.

"The Guess Who?"

A blank stare. "Any songs I might know?" she continued, still baffled.

"How about 'American Woman'?"

"Sorry," she smiled.

"'Undun'? 'These Eyes'? 'Laughing'?"

"Unh, unh."

"'Takin' Care of Business'? 'Let It Ride'? 'You Ain't Seen Nothing Yet'?"

"'You Ain't Seen Nothing Yet'?!" she exclaimed.

And with that she ran up to the pilot to tell him. He then proceeded to announce it to the entire plane and everyone fell over laughing because of the Smashy and Nicey skit. It's like Monty Python's "nudge nudge, wink wink" skit. Everybody knows it and loves it.

### LENNY KRAVITZ

When I first heard that retro-rocker Lenny Kravitz was covering "American Woman" for the movie soundtrack to *Austin Powers: The Spy Who Shagged Me,* I thought "Great!" I hadn't heard his version yet but I was excited because I like Lenny Kravitz. When he rocks, he has this incredible classic-rock sound, very Hendrix and Zeppelin. He's really into the old equipment and getting the authentic sound, as I am, using tube amps and an old board. He's become a diverse artist and in a Neil Young kind of way has charted his own course without trying to win favour with the latest pop trends. He has integrity.

When I received a copy of Lenny's version, though, I listened and kept waiting to hear my guitar riff, but it didn't come. "Did someone forget to mix it in? Was an amp turned off and no one noticed?" Then in came a lead guitar track playing a solo, a different kind of solo, so I knew they hadn't mixed the guitar out. I must admit that the first time I listened to it, I didn't like it. But after a few more listenings it started to grow on me and I realized the brilliance of Lenny's version. Other renditions of "American Woman," and covers of some of my other songs by artists, have always been identical clones of the original. As a writer you're flattered, yet there isn't another personality in it, so you don't really need to listen to it more than once. But here was Lenny Kravitz leaving out my guitar line, adding a key change, and putting his own stamp on the song. It's his interpretation of "American Woman," not simply a cover of it, and I appreciate that.

Lenny made "American Woman" contemporary. I'm continually amazed that my songs have longevity to them and keep reappearing. It proves that the music has transcended the generations and decades. For a songwriter it's terrific, an ongoing tribute to what you created.

The re-formed Guess Who played the MuchMusic Awards show in Toronto with Lenny and his band. They were these black New York dudes who dug hard rock. Lenny was extremely gracious to us all and very cool. He wanted the Guess Who to begin the song and he would join in.

"You're the guys who created it and did it first, and we're copying you, so you should start it."

"No," we told him. "What you did with the song was incredible. You should start it, and in the middle solo we'll just ease in and take it over. Then we can jam at the end and you and Burton can trade lines back and forth."

When we did it live it had so much energy, and the vibe between Lenny and us was incredible. He and Burton exchanged the vocal parts at the end back and forth, with Lenny mimicking Burton. That was definitely a highlight moment for us. What Lenny Kravitz did for our own status with contemporary rockers was extraordinary.

Afterwards, Lenny asked me for a Herzog to get that authentic "American Woman" guitar sound, so I asked Gar Gillies to make him one.

A while later I was getting a tour of the Rock 'n' Roll Hall of Fame in Cleveland and actor Denzel Washington was also there checking it out. When we were introduced, he was so excited to meet me that he picked up his cell phone and made a call. "Hey Lenny, you'll never 'Guess Who' I'm standing with at the Rock 'n' Roll Hall of Fame!"

### BARENAKED LADIES

I remember in the 50s as a little kid watching this TV show called *The Millionaire*. This rich, eccentric guy named John Beresford Tipton—what a regal-sounding name that is—would send his manservant or employee, whose name was Michael Anthony, to give some unsuspecting person a cheque for $1 million. Then it would show what they would do with the money. It was great to dream about that back then. We all used to play that game as kids: What would you do with a million dollars? Of course, for us back then $5 was a lot of money. You have to remember that in those days most parents were earning maybe $50 to $70 a week. As a teenager I could make $50 playing two nights. But my dad's generation believed that you had to work a legitimate job. Being a musician wasn't a real job to him. Only jazz musicians did that, and as far as he was concerned they were all drug addicts.

I was backstage with the Barenaked Ladies for a Canada Day show in 2008. I'd known them for several years and had played on other shows with them. So as we're hanging out backstage I asked Ed Robertson where he got the idea for the song "If I Had a Million Dollars." He told me that one summer he had a job as a camp counsellor and he had to keep the kids entertained and busy. One day he and the kids at this camp were sitting around and Ed told them he was a songwriter and asked if they wanted to help him write a song. "What should I write about?" he asked the kids. "Give me a song title and I'll see if I can write a song."

One kid says, "Why don't you write about what you'd do if you had a million dollars?" So all these kids start saying what they'd do with a million dollars, but because they're kids they say things like "I'd buy some new socks and shoes" or "I'd eat only Kraft Dinner" or "I'd buy a monkey." Ed took a lot of those ideas from the kids and with Steven Page wrote that song, which became a staple in their shows. It's a great song, a lot of fun.

The Barenaked Ladies and I are great friends and they've supported many of the same environmental causes that I have. We both played the Save the Stein Valley Festival when they were first getting started, and about ten years later they played at the Duncan, B.C., hockey arena with myself, my son Tal Bachman, and Neil Young for the Clean Air Concert. They put on a terrific show, as always.

### JANN ARDEN

I first met singer/songwriter Jann Arden in Calgary. I was at this classic rock radio station that's high up on a hill. I had a guitar with me and I'm playing songs and talking with the deejay. Other people are phoning in and talking with me on the air. Suddenly this girl calls in and says, "Stay there! Stay at the station. I'm coming down to see you." So as I'm coming out the front door after the radio show, this girl is driving up.

She jumps out of her car and says, "Here's a copy of my CD. I just think you're great, and I'm going to be great someday. I'm going to be big. I sent in my demo to A&M Records and have signed with them. I want you to have one of the first copies of my CD."

And I said, "Wow. What's your name, and I'll look for you."

"Jann Arden."

Well, soon afterwards she achieved what she had predicted. She's a great singer/songwriter, with nineteen Juno nominations and eight awards, including Songwriter of the Year, which even I couldn't do. Jann Arden wasn't kidding when she said she was going to be big. She's won multiple awards and accolades for songs such as "Insensitive," "Good Mother," and "Could I Be Your Girl." Yet she possesses a quick wit and a self-deprecating humour that has endeared her to fans and earned her a number of radio and television hosting roles. I've seen her live, and her shows are always wonderful and hilarious. She's so funny and entertaining.

### 9/11 AND CARNIE WILSON

The reunited Guess Who found ourselves in New York when the twin towers of the World Trade Center were hit. Touring plans had to be changed as travel was restricted. It would prove to be a life-altering event for me.

I was staying on the thirty-second floor of the Marriott Hotel overlooking Times Square in Manhattan the morning the World Trade Center was hit by those planes. The hotel looked right down the street to the World Trade Center. We were supposed to play New York, New Jersey, and Boston and then go home for a few days because we'd been together out on the road all summer. Our road manager, Marty Kramer, called me in my room early that morning and told me to turn on my television and look out my window. I could see the towers smoking and of course the story was all over the TV. It felt like the end of the world. I remember feeling numb and then terrified. My first thought was for my family and to phone home, but I couldn't get through to them because all the lines were either jammed or down. One of my kids got through on my cell phone and asked if I was okay. Finally my wife, Denise, got hold of me on the phone.

There were rumours flying around about bombs and other plots. It felt like a war zone.

Our manager, Lorne Saifer, called a contact in L.A. who had a brother in New Jersey who ran the shuttle service for Hertz Rent-a-Car. Arrangements were made for him to pick us up at the hotel the next day and take us to New Jersey where our driver, Rick Neufeld, was waiting with our tour bus.

There was no food and no service at the hotel. No trucks were getting in and the staff had either gone home or couldn't get in. So we had to hike through Times Square to find an open restaurant. Security was tight at the hotel, and I even had trouble getting back in again.

It was weird because we were walking along in the evening looking for an open restaurant and there was nothing on the street, not a car or a person. Broadway was empty; New York seemed deserted. Every restaurant said "Closed," so we just kept walking until we found an open deli with a big lineup out front full of celebrities who lived in downtown Manhattan. We had a three-hour wait in line, but we stayed and finally ate.

The next day the Hertz shuttle bus showed up to take us to New Jersey. We came down to the front doors of the Marriott with our guitars and suitcases. There were dozens of people standing there with their luggage. They had arrived but the hotel had closed and no one was able to get out to the airport, so these people were stranded there outside. Businessmen were desperate to get out. They're peeling off hundred-dollar bills asking, "Can you take me?" It was like a weird movie scene leaving New York. All these old trucks coming in to remove the debris from Ground Zero.

We just wanted to get back home to Canada, but couldn't. We couldn't get out of the U.S. We were stuck there on tour with Joe Cocker, so we just figured if the world's ending then let's just go out rocking. There was nothing else to do but embrace the music and each other and be glad we're alive and carry on. That was our attitude. Everyone thought in those early days after 9/11 that the attacks were going to continue and that America was going to go to war. It was like that movie *Independence Day*. It was a very surreal experience.

The New Jersey show was cancelled, so we headed up to Boston where we were scheduled to play a sold-out concert at the Tweeter Center. But only half the people showed up because they felt uneasy gathering in a large public place. People were still worried about more terrorist attacks. Security had to check everyone and every car before the show could start, which meant a two-hour delay. As a result, Joe Cocker did a half-hour and we did about forty minutes.

We weren't sure about playing "American Woman" that night because it has anti-American sentiments in it and we thought it might be inappropriate. We considered changing the lyrics. Some fans had emailed us telling us to change the lyrics to "Arab woman, stay away from me," but in the end we did it as is. As we played it I looked out over the audience and saw people standing on their seats, tears streaming down their faces. It was unbelievable.

When the tour resumed, I with my obsessive nature convinced myself that if this was going to be the end of the world, I was going to eat myself into oblivion. We were travelling long stretches on the tour bus and I'd be fuelling up at every truck stop, $20 or $30 worth of junk food. But with the angst going through my mind at the time, that food would be gone in twenty minutes. I was getting heavier and heavier, pushing 350, 360, 370 pounds. I was getting huge and I didn't care. Who knew if the world was going to end, so I'd have my last bucket of KFC, my last Wendy's burger, my last Long John Silver's ...

I desperately needed to lose weight. Once I hit 390 pounds I was like a refrigerator with a head, so I decided I had to do something. It was getting embarrassing going onstage being a huge guy in a rock 'n' roll band. It was a strange feeling trying to spread joy and rock the world when you're crying inside and you don't feel good about yourself. My weight was life-threatening.

I saw Carnie Wilson on shows like *Larry King Live* and *Oprah* talking about her gastric bypass surgery and how it had changed her life. Carnie is the eldest daughter of Beach Boys genius Brian Wilson, and with her sister Wendy and friend Chynna Phillips (daughter of the Mamas and Papas' John and Michelle Phillips) had scored a string of soft pop hits. Since then she'd become a spokesperson for weight loss, in particular gastric bypass surgery. Like me, Carnie had battled weight gain all her life and tried every diet on the market. None worked until she had the operation.

Like Carnie, I had a library full of every diet book there was, all of them working for about a month, after which I'd gain the weight back and more. It was that lifelong, up-and-down yo-yo weight syndrome and I suffered from it. I'd follow any new diet fad, and would call home saying things like, "Throw out all the food, I'm only going to eat pea pods and honey!" I once went for several months eating nothing but fruit. So I thought this operation might be the thing for me, too. I emailed Carnie Wilson and I got an answer back. To this day I've still never met her in person. She knew who I was because I'd toured with her dad and uncles. She sent me her doctor's name in San Diego and the name of the clinic where she had her bypass.

I researched the whole procedure and the history of it. It's done laparoscopically with a couple of small holes instead of a two-foot opening in your chest. I decided that this was the answer for me. So I booked into the clinic. There's an interview before they'll agree to do the surgery. You also have to meet with a psychiatrist. They don't want to do the procedure if all you're looking to do is go out and pick up twenty-year-old chicks. I wanted to live a long, productive life, active and rocking, because that's who I am and this is what I do.

I wanted the operation but I was scared, so I kept changing my mind. Then the clinic emailed me to say they had an opening on the U.S. Thanksgiving weekend, which is in late November. So I had to decide right then and there. A lot of people chicken out at the last minute because food has become their best friend. The guy who cancelled wanted to gorge himself over Thanksgiving and Christmas and then have the operation in the New Year. I had a day to make my decision.

I hadn't told Denise about any of this. Now I had to, and she was incredibly supportive. "I'll be there with you and help you through it." It's a major operation, and there's a recovery period of several weeks. So I went down to San Diego and had the operation.

The operation bypasses your stomach and creates a new little stomach the size of a golf ball that will expand as years go on. It's not really a stomach; it's part of your intestine they've pulled up. There's no digestion there. You have to do that with your mouth. I'd be full after just a little bit of food. I remember swallowing a vitamin pill early on and it felt like a brick. Your new stomach is very sensitive.

But it's the best thing I've ever done—it absolutely changed my life. I lost over 150 pounds. But there are rules you have to follow. You can't eat big portions and you have to chew your food well or you'll become violently ill. It's not a quick fix, though. There's a strict routine I have to adhere to, including regular exercise and dietary requirements. But I've gone from being Mr. Couch Potato to being the guy who can't wait to get up in the morning to go to the gym. And best of all I feel good, and good about myself again.

### GILES MARTIN

Travelling the world and sleeping in different beds almost every night, sitting on airplanes and sometimes jammed into tiny cars, I maintain a network of chiropractors around the world. (I travel with my own pillow now, which saves my neck.) It's very important for me not to have my back seize up. I've played sometimes with dislocated disks in my back and it ain't a good thing to do.

When I'm in London, England, I have a chiropractor there, Antoni Jakubowski, who's actually from British Columbia. I'm at his office in 2005 getting straightened out and he says to me, "There's a client of mine in the waiting room who's next to see me who's a fan of yours and would like to meet you. His name is Giles. He's a songwriter, too. He tried to hook up with you in Nashville a few years ago but was unable to." So after I get my back straight, I go out to the waiting room and there's this tall, stately looking gentleman there. I shake hands with him. I recognize him as a songwriter, nothing else. He asks me what I'm doing in London and I tell him I'm there to do some songwriting and a couple of shows.

"What are you doing now?" I ask him naively. "Are you still writing songs?"

He replies, "No, not really. I'm just kind of working with my dad on a musical project."

I still haven't caught on yet. "So what are you doing with your dad?"

He says, "It's kind of a love project."

So, still in the dark, I say to him, "Oh, so what does your dad do?"

Then he says, "He's George Martin. I'm Giles Martin."

Duh, what an idiot I am. His dad is Sir George Martin, the Beatles' record producer, Mr. Fifth Beatle. Giles invited me to the studio to hear some of the Beatles' *Love* album the two were working on for the big Cirque du Soleil Las Vegas production. For Beatles fans like me, who would have thought that in the new millennium we'd have a new Beatles album? I was choked up when I heard it. When I got the album, I sat there listening and crying. It's amazing.

Later, Giles invited me to Abbey Road Studios where he was transferring the Beatles' original tapes into the Pro Tools computer program for further work on their digital releases and iTunes. I sat there while he isolated each of the different Beatles voices and instruments for me, which all sounded quite eerie. But when he put all the tracks together it was this magical combination of individual genius that mesmerized the entire world and still does today. He then isolated each instrument in that famous opening chord to "A Hard Day's Night" for me. That blew me away.

## My Picks

"AMERICAN WOMAN" by Lenny Kravitz

"BOYS" by the Beatles

"CLASSICAL GAS" by Mason Williams

"COULD I BE YOUR GIRL" by Jann Arden

"FAITH" by George Michael

"GOTTA KEEP THE SUMMER ALIVE" by Union

"A HARD DAY'S NIGHT" by the Beatles

"I WANT CANDY" by the Strangeloves

"IF I HAD A MILLION DOLLARS" by Barenaked Ladies

"KEEP THE SUMMER ALIVE" by the Beach Boys

"LUCILLE" by Little Richard

"MY GENERATION" by the Who

"NIGHTS ON BROADWAY" by the Bee Gees

"PEACE TRAIN" by Cat Stevens

"PETER GUNN" by Henry Mancini

"PIECE OF MY HEART" by Big Brother and the Holding Company
(featuring Janis Joplin)

"RAISE A LITTLE HELL" by Trooper

"SHE WORKS HARD FOR THE MONEY" by Donna Summer

"SLOW HAND" by the Pointer Sisters

"SPANISH FLY" by Van Halen

"TAKE IT LIKE A MAN" by BTO

"TAKE THIS JOB AND SHOVE IT" by Johnny Paycheck

"THE THRILL IS GONE" by B.B. King

"THE TWIST" by Hank Ballard and the Midnighters

"WE'RE HERE FOR A GOOD TIME" by Trooper

"WHO DO YOU LOVE" by Bo Diddley

"WORKING MAN" by Rita MacNeil

"YOU AIN'T SEEN NOTHING YET" by BTO

# Conclusion

For as long as *Randy Bachman's Vinyl Tap* has been on the air, people have been asking for transcriptions of the shows. Well, I don't really have a script each week, I only work off a song list we prepare for that particular theme, and there's no time to write down what I've said. It's pretty much all off the cuff, either from my own knowledge or personal experience from five decades in the music business, or it's based on Denise's research.

When Penguin Canada approached me to do a *Randy Bachman's Vinyl Tap Stories* book, I was excited. It would allow me to tell many of my most memorable stories from the show and the fans would be able to download the songs from iTunes and put together their own package. I can't remember everything I said over six years, so I asked my writer friend John Einarson to help me out. I've known John since the 60s music scene in Winnipeg and he's written many great books on music. John plowed through hundreds of shows to pull out the best stories, and we worked together to compile song lists and theme lists. Presenting the oral stories in written form is not an easy thing. He's done an excellent job of sifting through the stories and compiling them into a readable format. I'm extremely pleased with the results and I hope listeners and readers will be, too. It's an opportunity to relive the *Vinyl Tap* experience and enjoy again the stories you liked best as well as the ones you might have missed.

One of my favourite things to do was to have friends over to my house and play them records I'd gathered from my travels all over the world and explain to them what was intriguing or different about each one. Now I get to do that every weekend with millions of people. Last year at a gig where the Canadian classic rock band Lighthouse opened for me, keyboard player Paul Hoffert said, "Isn't it interesting that you've travelled, played music, and done research for this show for the past forty years?" He was right.

I love doing *Vinyl Tap* because it reminds me of how and why I love so many different kinds of music. It has also opened my world up to so many new friends who listen every week and contact us. From all the feedback and mail we receive, our listeners range in age from eight to eighty and come from the most amazing places in the world.

I also appreciate the fact that CBC Radio is commercial-free and gives me the freedom to play whatever music I want. What I like the most, though, is trying to find and play songs like the radio I listened to growing up, a very eclectic mix of styles and sounds. What a great mixture it was.

Cheers.

# Randy's Favourites

On *Vinyl Tap*, once I got into the swing of "theme" shows featuring songs over a span of five decades that have the same subject matter or some other connection, the fans began responding with theme ideas of their own as well as providing us with song lists to start each idea rolling. Denise and I would go through the song lists, add some of our own ideas, and eventually come up with a show. Most of the show has to be music that I like and am familiar with so that I can talk about it and hopefully relay a personal experience or connection to the song that will be interesting to the listeners. I now have enough theme ideas for many years of shows, and they keep coming in. Some of them, like funeral songs, for example— I never would have thought of that theme for *Vinyl Tap*—really surprise me and are great. I can't wait to get at them and get the shows ready.

## RANDY'S FAVOURITE DOUBLE A-SIDED SINGLES

With CDs, MP3s, iTunes, and digital downloads, talking about A- and B-sides of a record no longer applies. But wasn't it great when you got two A-sides, or top songs, on one record instead of a B-side for your 99¢? The Beatles, the Stones, Creedence, and even the Guess Who had several double A-sided hits. Not an easy thing to accomplish, but if you did, it was quite something. The Guess Who are in some pretty impressive company.

1  The Beatles: Penny Lane / Strawberry Fields Forever

2  Queen: We Will Rock You / We Are the Champions

3  The Rolling Stones:   Honky Tonk Women / You Can't Always Get What You Want

4  Creedence Clearwater Revival: Proud Mary / Born on the Bayou

5  The Beach Boys: I Get Around / Don't Worry Baby

6  Rod Stewart: Reason to Believe / Maggie May

7  The Guess Who: American Woman / No Sugar Tonight

8  The Everly Brothers: All I Have to Do Is Dream / Claudette

9  The Beatles: Day Tripper / We Can Work It Out

10  Elvis Presley: Hound Dog / Don't Be Cruel

11  The Guess Who: Laughing / Undun

12  Larry Williams: Slow Down / Dizzy Miss Lizzie

13  Little Richard: Rip It Up / Ready Teddy

14  Bobby Day: Rockin' Robin / Over and Over

### RANDY'S 25 FAVOURITE GIRL GROUP SONGS

Girl groups were quite a phenomenon in the 1960s. Every song was sing-along material and each song was a step up from the simple but repetitive doo-wop songs of the 50s. Just reading the titles below, you instantly start singing the choruses in your head. That's how ingrained in our consciousness these songs are. Most of the girl group songs came from either New York's Brill Building or Motown (Detroit) and have stood the test of time. I got to perform with and even back up many of the New York girl groups like the Crystals, the Shirelles, the Ronettes, Candy and the Kisses, and more. They were all great people, fun to work with, and their music lives on.

1  Be My Baby—the Ronettes

2  He's So Fine—the Chiffons

3  Leader of the Pack—the Shangri-Las

4  Will You Still Love Me Tomorrow—the Shirelles

5  Heat Wave—Martha and the Vandellas

6  My Boyfriend's Back—the Angels

7  Maybe—the Chantels

8  Tell Him—the Exciters

9  Chains—the Cookies

10  Chapel of Love—the Dixie Cups

11  Dancing in the Streets—Martha and the Vandellas

12  Don't Say Nothin' Bad About My Baby—the Cookies

**13** One Fine Day—the Chiffons

**14** A Lover's Concerto—the Toys

**15** Boogie Woogie Bugle Boy—the Andrews Sisters

**16** Sugartime—the McGuire Sisters

**17** Stop! In the Name of Love—the Supremes

**18** Quicksand—Martha and the Vandellas

**19** He's a Rebel—the Crystals

**20** Da Doo Ron Ron—the Crystals

**21** Baby It's You—the Shirelles

**22** Please Mr. Postman—the Marvelettes

**23** Mr. Lee—the Bobbettes

**24** Tonight You Belong to Me—Patience and Prudence

**25** He's a Doll—the Honeys

## RANDY'S 10 FAVOURITE COWBELL SONGS

After seeing a repeat of the "More Cowbell" skit on *Saturday Night Live,* my whole band and Kevin Duffy, my road manager, said, "How about a *Vinyl Tap* show on the cowbell?" It wasn't hard to put together. We made a list right away. I started out the show telling the audience to get something to bang on because they could participate in this with a spoon and a pot, or a fork and a bottle. The show was a big success. To this day I'll be walking down the street in Toronto, Winnipeg, Vancouver, or anywhere and someone will roll down the car or truck window and yell out, "We loved the cowbell show!" So thanks to *Saturday Night Live* for that great skit, and everyone who played along at home.

1  (Don't Fear) The Reaper—Blue Öyster Cult

2  Drive My Car—the Beatles

3  All Right Now—Free

4  Honky Tonk Women—the Rolling Stones

5  We're an American Band—Grand Funk Railroad

6  Oye Como Va—Santana

7  Down on the Corner—Creedence Clearwater Revival

8  Free Ride—the Edgar Winter Group

9  Time Has Come Today—the Chambers Brothers

10  You Ain't Seen Nothing Yet—BTO

### RANDY'S 10 FAVOURITE ROCK 'N' ROLL MONDEGREENS

Mondegreens are misheard or misinterpreted lyrics. What you think you hear may not be what the songwriter actually wrote. That's the fun part of mondegreens, what you think someone is really singing. The word comes from a seventeenth-century ballad where the line "And laid him on the green" was misinterpreted as "And Lady Mondegreen." Denise came up with this theme, and it was one of our more popular shows. I have a ton of my own favourite mondegreens, but it was great to get listener feedback and their own misheard words. One of my faves was "baking carrot biscuits" for "Taking Care of Business."

**1** Purple Haze—Jimi Hendrix:
"'Scuse me while I kiss this guy"
(actual lyric: "'Scuse me while I kiss the sky")

**2** Bad Moon Rising—Creedence Clearwater Revival:
"There's a bathroom on the right"
(actual lyric: "There's a bad moon on the rise")

**3** Lucy in the Sky with Diamonds—the Beatles:
"The girl with colitis goes by"
(actual lyric: "The girl with kaleidoscope eyes")

**4** Rocket Man—Elton John:
"Burning all the shoes off everyone"
(actual lyric: "Rocket man, burning out his fuse up here alone")

**5** Groovin'—the Young Rascals:
"You and me and Leslie groovin'"
(actual lyric: "You and me, endlessly groovin'")

**6** Secret Agent Man—Johnny Rivers:
"Secret Asian man"
(actual lyric: "Secret agent man")

**7**  The Heart of Rock 'n' Roll—Huey Lewis and the News:
"The harder rock 'n' roll is in Cleveland"
(actual lyric: "Heart of rock and roll is still beating")

**8**   Tiny Dancer—Elton John:
"Hold me closer Tony Danza"
(actual lyric: "Hold me closer tiny dancer")

**9**  You're the One That I Want—John Travolta and Olivia
Newton-John:
"I've got shoes, they're made of plywood"
(actual lyric: "I've got chills, they're multiplyin'")

**10**  Another Brick in the Wall—Pink Floyd:
"No Dukes of Hazzard in the classroom"
(actual lyric: "No dark sarcasm in the classroom")

**SONGS PLAYED AT YOUR FUNERAL**

It was amazing to get the listeners' views on this subject. Some
were seriously sad and some were very funny, ranging from "Our
Leaves Are Green Again" to "Another One Bites the Dust" and
"Wasn't That a Party." Everyone loved this show, and it also made
many put the music requests into their last will and testament.

1  I Shall Be Released—the Band

2  And When I Die—Blood Sweat & Tears

3  Peaceful Easy Feeling—the Eagles

4  Two of Us—the Beatles

5  Old and Wise—the Alan Parsons Project

6  Friends in Low Places—Garth Brooks

7  Bridge Over Troubled Waters—Simon & Garfunkel

8  I Will Remember You—Sarah McLachlan

9  Wasn't That a Party—the Irish Rovers

10  Spirit in the Sky—Norman Greenbaum

11  All My Tears—Emmylou Harris

12  Precious Time—Van Morrison

13  Without You—Harry Nilsson

14  Thank U—Alanis Morissette

15  When I Die—Motherlode

## RANDY'S 15 FAVOURITE CHUCK BERRY SONGS

Chuck Berry is unquestionably the greatest storyteller in rock 'n' roll. He knew what teenagers thought and he wrote songs that captured those thoughts and images. Every song painted a picture in your mind with a great storyline. Chuck even made up his own words to fill a rhyme, and we understood the word the first time we heard it, like the word "motorvatin'" in the song "Maybellene." I've taken to doing that as well with words I've put together, like gi-normous, huge-antic, and others. But there was no one like Chuck Berry.

1  Johnny B. Goode

2  Roll Over Beethoven

3  Maybellene

4  Rock and Roll Music

5  Sweet Little Sixteen

6  Too Much Monkey Business

7  School Days

8  Reelin' and Rockin'

9  Nadine

10  Brown Eyed Handsome Man

11  Little Queenie

**12**  No Particular Place to Go

**13**  Promised Land

**14**  You Never Can Tell

**15**  Memphis, Tennessee

.

## RANDY'S 25 FAVOURITE VEHICLE SONGS

All these songs get your motor runnin', whether it's in a car, truck, or motorcycle.

**1**  She Loves My Automobile—ZZ Top (with Willie Nelson)

**2**  Crawling from the Wreckage—Dave Edmunds

**3**  Maybellene—Chuck Berry

**4**  Hot Rod Race—Arkie Shibley

**5**  409—the Beach Boys

**6**  Who Drove the Red Sports Car—Van Morrison

**7**  Souped-Up Ford—Rory Gallagher

**8**  Hot Rod Lincoln—Johnny Bond

**9**  The Boys in the Bright White Sports Car—Trooper

**10**  Somethin' Else—Eddie Cochran

**11**  Little Deuce Coupe—the Beach Boys

**12**  Rocket 88—Jackie Brenston and His Delta Cats

**13**  Cars—Gary Numan

**14**  Radar Love—Golden Earring

**15**  I'm in Love with My Car—Roger Taylor (Queen)

**16**  Fun, Fun, Fun—the Beach Boys

**17**  Dead Man's Curve—Jan and Dean

**18** Drive My Car—the Beatles

**19** Seven Little Girls Sitting in the Back Seat—Paul Evans

**20** Mercedes Benz—Janis Joplin

**21** I Drove All Night—Roy Orbison (also Celine Dion)

**22** Born to Be Wild—Steppenwolf

**23** The Little Old Lady from Pasadena—Jan and Dean

**24** Teen Angel—Mark Dinning

**25** (I'm Your) Vehicle—the Ides of March

## RANDY'S 25 FAVOURITE INSTRUMENTAL POP SONGS

Instrumentals are very important. They're all about melody. You know how in real estate they say the three most important factors in looking for a house are location, location, location? Well, in songwriting it's melody, melody, melody. Many great songs first came to life as melody or an instrumental before someone put lyrics to them. Then the song takes on a new life. But a good instrumental melody can live on forever because it sticks in people's brains.

**1** Let's Go—the Routers

**2** Let There Be Drums—Sandy Nelson

**3** Pipeline—the Surfaris

**4** Wonderful Land—the Shadows

**5** Tequila—the Champs

**6** Green Onions—Booker T. and the MGs

**7** Honky Tonk (Parts 1 & 2)—Bill Doggett

**8** Man of Mystery—the Shadows

**9** Rawhide—Link Wray

**10** Rock and Roll (Part 2)—Gary Glitter and the Glitter Band

**11** Telstar—the Tornados

**12** Forty Miles of Bad Road—Duane Eddy

**13** Ramrod—Duane Eddy

**14** Atlantis—Mark Knopfler

**15** 7-11 (Mambo No. 5)—Gone All Stars

**16** Miserlou—Dick Dale

**17** Torquay—the Fireballs

**18** Like, Long Hair—Paul Revere and the Raiders

**19** Guitar Boogie Shuffle—the Virtues

**20** Gonzo—James Booker

**21** Last Night—the Mar-Keys

**22** Penetration—the Pyramids

**23** Freeway Jam—Jeff Beck

**24** 77 Sunset Strip—Warren Barker

**25** Train to Nowhere—the Champs

## RANDY'S 20 FAVOURITE FOOD SONGS

The food-song theme was suggested by one of our listeners. We didn't want it to be instrumentals, we wanted the food name in the lyrics as well as the title. Denise did the research on this one because many of these songs were hard to find. But we told listeners to get out some of their favourite foods and eat along with the show because the songs were bound to make them all hungry.

1  Jambalaya—Jeff Healey

2  Bread and Butter—The Newbeats

3  Mashed Potato Time—Dee Dee Sharp

4  Gravy (For My Mashed Potatoes)—Dee Dee Sharp

5  Dixie Chicken—Little Feat

6  Peaches—the Presidents of the United States of America

7  The Banana Boat Song—Harry Belafonte

8  Cheeseburger in Paradise—Jimmy Buffett

9  Catfish Blues—the Jimi Hendrix Experience

10  Peanuts—Little Joe and the Thrillers

11  One Bad Apple—the Osmonds

12  Watermelon Man—Mongo Santamaria

13  Hambone—Red Saunders and His Orchestra with Delores Saunders and the Hambone Kids

**14**  Cherry Pie—Warrant

**15**  Cherry Pie—Skip and Flip

**16**  I Want Candy—the Strangeloves

**17**  Blueberry Hill—Fats Domino

**18**  Ice Cream—Sarah McLachlan

**19**  Peanut Butter—the Vibrations

**20**  No Sugar Tonight—the Guess Who

## RANDY'S 25 FAVOURITE ONE-HIT WONDERS

I was one of these for a short period of time and I'm so glad that I'm not anymore: a one-hit wonder. You work hard learning your instrument, getting a band together, writing songs, recording, praying, hoping, and trying to have a hit. And when you do you're a one-hit wonder until you can find that magic formula to follow it up. It's often said that you're only as good as your last record, and following up a big hit can be extremely difficult. The recording artists listed below were unable, for whatever reason, to follow up their one hit with another hit. They may have enjoyed a wonderful career without another hit. At least they got that one hit; plenty of recording artists never even get that. People may not recognize the name of the band or singer, but as soon as you say the name of the record or sing a bit of it they go, "Oh, that song!"

**1**  99 Luftballons (Red Balloons)—Nena

**2**  Just the Way It Is, Baby—the Rembrandts

**3**  Breakfast at Tiffany's—Deep Blue Something

**4**  (I Just) Died in Your Arms Tonight—Cutting Crew

**5**  Venus—Shocking Blue

**6**  Harlem Shuffle—Bob and Earl

**7**  Spirit in the Sky—Norman Greenbaum

**8**  Something in the Air—Thunderclap Newman

**9**  Fire—the Crazy World of Arthur Brown

**10**  Runaway Train—Soul Asylum

**11** Your Woman—White Town

**12** Ride Captain Ride—Blues Image

**13** Mississippi Queen—Mountain

**14** Come On Eileen—Dexy's Midnight Runners

**15** Tainted Love—Soft Cell

**16** As the Years Go By—Mashmakhan

**17** Hey! Baby—Bruce Channel

**18** Achy Breaky Heart—Billy Ray Cyrus

**19** Wild Weekend—the Rebels

**20** Pretty Little Angel Eyes—Curtis Lee

**21** Sukiyaki—Kyu Sakamoto

**22** Have I the Right?—the Honeycombs

**23** Tobacco Road—the Nashville Teens

**24** Just Like Romeo and Juliet—the Reflections

**25** Elusive Butterfly—Bob Lind

## RANDY'S 25 FAVOURITE NOVELTY SONGS

There are hardly any novelty songs released anymore, but back in the 1950s, 60s, and 70s they were all the rage: novelty songs with trick voices, sound effects, spoofs of other songs, etc., and plenty of fun and good melodies. Today they're on children's CDs, but back then they were hit records. Many people sent in a request for a show about these kinds of songs. I certainly remembered them all and had fun playing them.

1  We're a Ukrainian Band—Bob Rivers

2  Itsy Bitsy Teenie Weenie Yellow Polka Dot Bikini—Brian Hyland

3  The Purple People Eater—Sheb Wooley

4  They're Coming to Take Me Away—Napoleon XIV

5  Disco Duck—Rick Dees

6  Witch Doctor—David Seville

7  Boogie Bear—Boyd Bennett

8  Pretty Blue Eyes (bad version)—the Guess Who

9  Monster Mash—Bobby "Boris" Pickett

10  Does Your Chewing Gum Lose Its Flavour (On the Bedpost Overnight?)—Lonnie Donegan

11  Clean the Aquarium—Bob Rivers

12  Hello Mudduh, Hello Fadduh—Allan Sherman

13  The Banana Boat Song—Stan Freberg

**14** Tiptoe Through the Tulips—Tiny Tim

**15** King Tut—Steve Martin

**16** A Hard Day's Night—Peter Sellers

**17** The Hockey Song—Stompin' Tom Connors

**18** Peaches—the Presidents of the United States of America

**19** Fish Heads—Barnes and Barnes

**20** The Name Game—Shirley Ellis

**21** Valley Girl—Frank Zappa (with Moon Unit Zappa)

**22** Tie Me Kangaroo Down, Sport—Rolf Harris

**23** Mr. Custer—Larry Verne

**24** I Put a Spell on You—Screamin' Jay Hawkins

**25** Convoy—C.W. McCall

**RANDY'S FAVOURITE SONGS WITH GIRLS' NAMES IN THE TITLE**

When I did a show on songs with guys' names in the title, we had a tough time finding enough songs to fill the two hours. But with girls' names we had to do two shows and still had plenty more to choose from … except, of course, for the letter X. Does *Xena: Warrior Princess* have a theme song?

**A**    Alison—Elvis Costello
      Annie's Song—John Denver
      Polk Salad Annie—Tony Joe White

**B**    Barbara Ann—the Beach Boys
      Bernadette—the Four Tops
      Billy Jean—Michael Jackson
      Bony Moronie—Larry Williams

**C**    Carol—Chuck Berry
      Cathy's Clown—Everly Brothers
      Claudette—Everly Brothers
      Oh! Carol—Neil Sedaka

**D**    Denise—Fountains of Wayne
      Denise—Randy and the Rainbows
      Diana—Paul Anka
      Dolly Dagger—Jimi Hendrix
      Donna—Ritchie Valens

**E**    Come On Eileen—Dexy's Midnight Runners
      Eleanor Rigby—the Beatles

**F**    Fannie Mae—Buster Brown
      Short Fat Fannie—Larry Williams

**G**  Gloria—Laura Branigan
Gloria—Them (with Van Morrison)
Guinnevere—Crosby, Stills and Nash

**H**  Helen Wheels—Paul McCartney and Wings
Holly Holy—Neil Diamond

**I**  Goodnight, Irene—the Weavers
Irene Wilde—Ian Hunter
Izabella—Jimi Hendrix

**J**  Jane—Barenaked Ladies
Jennifer Juniper—Donovan
Jolene—Dolly Parton
Judy in Disguise—John Fred and His Playboy Band
Lady Jane—the Rolling Stones

**K**  Kate—Ben Folds Five
Kathy's Song—Simon & Garfunkel

**L**  Dizzy Miss Lizzy—Larry Williams
Layla—Derek and the Dominoes (Eric Clapton)
Linda Lu—Ray Sharpe
Lola—the Kinks
Lucille—Little Richard
Lucy in the Sky with Diamonds—the Beatles
Pictures of Lily—the Who

**M**  Along Comes Mary—the Association
Hello Mary Lou—Ricky Nelson
Lady Madonna—the Beatles
Maggie May—Rod Stewart
Maybellene—Chuck Berry
Michelle—the Beatles
Proud Mary—Creedence Clearwater Revival

**N**   Nadine—Chuck Berry

**O**   Ophelia—the Band

**P**   Hey Paula—Paul and Paula
        Palmyra—the Guess Who
        Peggy Sue—Buddy Holly

**Q**   Little Queenie—Chuck Berry

**R**   Help Me, Rhonda—the Beach Boys
        Rosanna—Toto
        Roxanne—the Police
        Ruby Tuesday—the Rolling Stones
        Walk Away Renée—the Left Banke

**S**   Mustang Sally—Wilson Pickett
        Runaround Sue—Dion and the Belmonts
        Sara—Fleetwood Mac
        Sara Smile—Hall and Oates
        Susie Q—Dale Hawkins
        Wake Up Little Susie—Everly Brothers

**T**   Tammy—Debbie Reynolds
        Tracy—the Cuff Links

**U**   Ursula—Barclay James Harvest

**V**   Valerie—Steve Winwood
        Valleri—the Monkees
        Venus—Frankie Avalon
        Veronica—Elvis Costello
        Victoria—the Kinks

**W**   Wendy—the Beach Boys
        Windy—the Association

**X** ? (Is there a song with a girl's name starting with X?)

**Y** Dear Yoko—John Lennon and Yoko Ono
Yolanda—Alfie Zappacosta

**Z** Zoe—Eminem

# *Acknowledgments*

I would like to express my sincere thanks to the following: Denise McCann Bachman for her support, creative input, and handling of all the mail so diligently; my manager Gilles Paquin in Winnipeg; *Vinyl Tap* producer Tod Elvidge; Chris Boyce for helping me formulate the early *Vinyl Tap* shows and create the template; Jon Conrad at Bachman Headquarters; Jennifer McGuire at CBC Radio for taking a chance on me as a radio host; Denise Donlon, the new head of CBC Radio, who encouraged me to keep the Rock Rollin'; Diane Turbide and Justin Stoller at Penguin Canada for their dedication to seeing this project through; my old friend, writer John Einarson, for all his research; to the listeners all over the world who tune in each week to *Randy Bachman's Vinyl Tap*; and to my fans who have supported all my musical endeavours over the years. "If there ain't no audience, there ain't no show!"

Rock on!
*Randy Bachman*

# *Index*